SAS

THE WORLD'S BEST

SIDGWICK & JACKSON
LONDON

SAS

THE WORLD'S BEST

**PETER
DARMAN**

First published in Great Britain in 1994
by Sidgwick & Jackson Limited
A division of Macmillan General Books
Cavaye Place, London SW10 9PG
and Basingstoke

ISBN 0 283 06222 3

Printed and bound in Great Britain by
BPC Hazell Books Ltd
A member of
The British Printing Company Ltd

Editorial and Design: Brown Packaging

1 3 5 7 9 8 6 4 2

Picture credits

Australian Defence Force: 11, 19, 77, 93,
106/7, 129, 173; **Aviation Photographs
International:** 98, 122; **Brown Packaging:** 16,
39, 40/1, 49, 57, 63, 74, 79, 139, 144, 147, 148,
150/1, 153, 154, 155, 157, 167, 175;
Bundesministerium der Verteidigung, Bonn:
58; **Federal Bureau of Investigation:** 140;
Israeli Defense Forces: 17, 80, 117, 180;
Headquarters, Republic of Korea Army: 24;
Bob Morrison's Military Scene: 32/3; **Royal
Netherlands Marine Corp:** 64, 124; **New
Zealand M.o.D.:** 10; **Photo Press:** 2/3, 6/7, 18,
26/7, 46/7, 52/3, 54/5, 59, 86/87, 92, 94, 100/1,
103, 110, 114, 118/9, 120/1, 128, 136/7, 142, 143,
170/1, back cover; **Anthony Rogers:** 20/1, 37;
Soldier Magazine: 84, 135; **Souter Composites
Ltd.:** 112; **Headquarters, Spanish Foreign
Legion:** 29, 30; **SAS Association:** 68, 69; **Frank
Spooner Pictures:** 71; **TRH Pictures:** 9, 35, 45,
67, 75, 78, 88, 90, 91, 97, 99, 111, 125, 126,
130/1, 132/3, 158/9, 160, 162, 163, 164, 166, 172,
182/3; **Thorn EMI:** 83; **United States D.o.D.:**
13, 14, 23, 36, 42, 48, 61, 72/3, 104, 105, 109,
176/7, 178/9; **United States National Archives:**
50, 169

**Previous pages: A British special forces parachutist
photographed during a HALO descent.
Back cover: The marks of excellence: the SAS's
winged dagger badge and beige beret.**

CONTENTS

SELECTION & TRAINING

Selection courses for the world's elite forces are designed to ensure that only those who have the right qualities get through. The toughest is that for the SAS, but others come very close.

This chapter will compare the SAS's selection and training programmes with those of other elite units around the world to determine whether SAS training methods produce better soldiers than do those of other special forces units. The comparison will be made on a number of levels. First, how entry qualifications compare; second, the selection courses themselves; third, the post-selection training given to individuals; and fourth, any advanced training that is given to individuals.

Comparing the SAS with other elite units is, in many ways, futile, because different units have different tasks. For example, the mountain troops of Germany, France and Italy are well trained, but alpine troops are only tasked with being mountain infantry – no more and no less. However, all elite units conduct rigorous selection and training courses, and many of these courses are similar in content. But first, it would be useful to compare the wartime roles of the SAS with those of other units, to put training courses in context.

All over the world, special forces units devote a great deal of effort to attracting suitable raw material and training it up

Volunteers on SAS Selection tramp over the Brecon Beacons. The course is designed to test physical and mental endurance, and is reckoned the world's toughest.

to the highest standards: none is more rigorous in its selection process than the British SAS.

The British SAS has a wide variety of wartime roles, such as intelligence gathering, counter-insurgency warfare, raids, ambushes, behind-the-lines operations and a whole host of missions associated with long-range reconnaissance skills. In addition, it has a counter-terrorist and hostage-rescue brief. All these roles have to be carried out by a unit that has around 350 'badged' (fully qualified) personnel; it necessarily follows that each man must possess a multitude of skills.

The Cold War determined the role of the majority of Europe's elite units

The Australian SAS's role, on the other hand, is associated mainly with long-range reconnaissance, plus counter-terrorism, while the New Zealand SAS's primary role is counter-terrorism (the unit, which has only one squadron of regulars, has very little long-range insertion/-extraction assets to support foreign operations).

American elite units tend to have a narrower band of roles. The Green Berets, for example, are primarily concerned with teaching and organising friendly guerrilla groups and countries to defend themselves against anti-American insurgency (the threat of communism has now largely given way to the dangers of Islamic fundamentalism). The US Navy's Sea-Air-Land (SEAL) teams are tasked with clandestine scouting of enemy coasts, harbours and inshore waters and raiding, while SEAL Team 6 is tasked with hostage-rescue. Long-range reconnaissance and other elite infantry tasks are the preserve of the US Army's Rangers.

The Canadian Special Service Force is a highly mobile, self-contained army that is responsible for maintaining a territorial defence force, and also provides aid during major air disasters and support for counter-terrorist operations. Like the SAS, it has a wide variety of roles, but it is an army and different branches fulfil different roles (individuals do not have to be as multi-skilled as SAS soldiers).

The Cold War between NATO and the Warsaw Pact, in the years between the end of

World War II and the break-up of the Soviet Union and Warsaw Pact at the end of the 1980s, determined the role of most of western Europe's elite units, which were, in the main, tasked with being rapid deployment forces to counter any Warsaw Pact invasion of western Europe. For some this was their only role. For example, French, German and Italian mountain troops were expected to fight Soviet and east European forces in a conventional war setting. Units such as Spain's Legion, Britain's Parachute Regiment and Royal Marines, France's Foreign Legion, Belgium's Para-Commandos and Holland's Marine Corps were also, and still are, rapid reaction units. However, some of them, like the British Paras, Royal Marines, French Foreign Legion and Spanish Legion, also had, and still have, an 'Out of Area' role (a term that usually denotes operations outside NATO's central command area, i.e. western Europe).

With the collapse of the Soviet Union and the Warsaw Pact, 'Out of Area' operations have become a higher priority for Western elite units than ever before, and the 1991 Gulf War between Iraq and the United Nations witnessed the deployment of a number of European and US elite units to Arabia. These included the British SAS and Special Boat Service (the special operations unit of the Royal Marines), the French Foreign Legion, and the US SEALs and Green Berets.

Spetsnaz was to have spearheaded any Warsaw Pact aggression in Europe

The Russian elite unit Spetsnaz had a slightly different role from that of its Western counterparts: while Western forces were defensive and reactive, Spetsnaz was to have spearheaded any Warsaw Pact aggression in central Europe. Its tasks were clandestine scouting, reconnaissance, sabotage, assassination and general guerrilla and destabilising operations. The Spetsnaz role is now more defensive in nature, but the organisation is still capable of offensive action should the need arise.

The elite units outside the European theatre, excluding North America, tailored their

Above: The early days. Recruits train at the first SAS camp, at Kabrit in Egypt, in the North African desert during World War II. David Stirling insisted on a high level of fitness.

role to their specific theatres of operation. However, they all possessed one or more of the qualities that are associated with elite forces: some were parachute-trained (Indian Para-Commandos, Jordanian 101st Special Forces and Israeli Paras), others specialised in reconnaissance (Israeli sayeret units, Royal Thai Special Forces, South African Recce Commandos and Oman's Independent Reconnaissance Regiment), while others had a counter-terrorist capability (Indian Para-Commandos and Pakistan's Army Special Service Group).

Whatever the role of an elite unit, however, its personnel must attain a high physical and mental standard. Consequently, special forces organisations have a number of entry requirements that will, they hope, ensure that the men coming forward are of the right calibre to be turned into elite soldiers. This is the first hurdle a man must pass on his way to membership of a special forces unit. The entry qualifications for selection form the first level of comparison between the SAS and other elite units.

The first step a man must take if he wants to join an elite unit is to volunteer himself for selection. There are very few special forces units that enlist conscripts into their ranks. Those that do, such as the Belgian Para-Commandos, the German Mountain Troops, Spetsnaz, the Israeli Golani Brigade and the Italian Alpine Troops, are looking for outstanding recruits who have an aptitude for the unit's specific role. However, taking conscripts must be considered a major weakness. After all, a man who puts himself forward will be far more motivated to succeed than one who is 'pushed'.

It is impossible to enter the Special Air Service directly

Those who wish to join the SAS must fulfil certain criteria in order to be eligible for Selection Training. First, they must have served with a regular corps or regiment and gained a good grounding in their corps or regimental skills. In this the SAS has an advantage, i.e. it only takes men who have had prior military service. Volunteers for the SAS come from all arms and corps of the British Army, and also, in smaller numbers, from the RAF (mainly the RAF Regiment). Second, they must have a minimum of three years and three months left to serve from the date they pass Selection.

Because it is impossible to enter the SAS directly, recruits tend to be in their mid-20s. This means they are more mature, both physically and mentally, than their teenage counterparts in other, conventional, units, as well as those recruits to other elite units. In the Australian SAS there is a wider age spread, with recruits ranging between the late teens and early 30s, though every recruit must first have served with his parent unit.

Royal Marines wishing to become members of the Special Boat Service (SBS) face a pre-selection course. The Junior Command Course, combined with physical, trade and aptitude tests, is conducted at the SBS's headquarters at Poole in Dorset. It lasts for two weeks and is designed to weed out the poorly motivated. The course starts with a timed 32km endurance walk carrying a 23kg bergen (backpack). Upon completion of this march, the successful candidates face a night in the open, alone and without any survival gear. Next morning they undertake a 48km endurance walk (these walks include unexpected river crossings, which

Above: A New Zealand SAS trooper begins a freefall parachute descent. The main role of New Zealand's elite is counter-terrorism.

require the men to swim with their bergens). Confidence in the water is also tested when the men are asked to swim with their equipment to a landing craft moored 0.5km offshore. For those who succeed, the rest of pre-selection is spent testing their suitability for diving.

Volunteers for the US Rangers can be civilian volunteers who need only have passed the Army Readiness Test (push-ups, sit-ups and a 3km run – all timed). Because the entry requirement is relatively undemanding, the average age of recruits is usually between 18 and 19. Compared to the aspiring SAS recruits, they are of a lower standard. The Green Berets and SEALs, on the other hand, have higher entry qualifications than the SAS. Volunteers for the Green Berets must be airborne-qualified, high school graduates. They must have passed Basic Training, Advanced Individual Training (Military Occupation Speciality), the Advanced Physical Readiness Test and the junior NCO's

course. In addition, they must be able to swim 50m in boots and uniform.

Volunteers for the SEALs must be specialised in at least one area of expertise, such as medical care, engineering or electronics. They must pass a rigorous diving medical and produce high scores in both physical and mental aptitude tests. Because it takes a long time to gain the experience needed to satisfy the strict entry requirements, recruits for both the SEALs and Green Berets, like the SAS, are usually in their mid-20s.

Besides the SAS and SBS, European units tend to have less stringent entry qualifications, and some, such as the British Paras, Spanish Legion, French Foreign Legion and Belgian Para-Commandos, have none at all apart from assessing the recruit as physically and mentally capable. These units all tend to work on the 'many are called, few are chosen' philosophy, in the belief that training will almost immediately sift out those who are unsuitable.

In other parts of the world, elite units have very tough entry qualifications, and some more demanding than the SAS. For example, recruits for the South Korean 'Capital Command' must have a good education and be proficient in martial arts (Koreans believe both qualities are indicators of whether an individual will make the grade); the Royal Thai Special Forces demand that their recruits have high educational standards and have completed both the Ranger Course (run by the Thai Special Warfare Center) and Airborne Training.

The Jesuits have a saying: 'Give me a child until he is seven and he will be a Catholic for the rest of his life'. The authorities in the former Soviet Union echoed these sentiments, except that they applied the doctrine to loyalty to the USSR and the ideology of communism.

The start of the process that could result in a child becoming a Spetsnaz soldier began before the age of 10, when he or she joined the Octobrists (a youth organisation that taught simplistically about the Red Army and communism). The youngster would then progress through the Pioneers (where they would receive more advanced indoctrination),

zarnitsa (summer lightning) camps (under the watchful eye of retired military officers), Komsomol (Young Communist League), *orlyonok* (little eagle) camps (to develop skills in map reading and weapons handling), and DOSAFF (Voluntary Society for Cooperation with the Army, Air Force and Navy), before being conscripted into the Soviet Special Forces.

Though the Soviet Union has collapsed, many of the former communist youth organisations remain, and they continue to be used as preparation for service in the armed forces in general and Spetsnaz in particular. Youngsters are still encouraged to view Russia as an island surrounded by potential enemies, and the need for eternal vigilance is impressed upon them. By the time they are eligible for the draft, they will have the correct mental attitude towards military service, as well as having a

Below: Volunteers on Australian SAS Selection check their bearings. Navigation skills are developed by such exercises in the 'outback'.

grounding in drills and tactics. It is extremely thorough pre-military training.

Prospective members of the Indian Para-Commandos are drawn from outstanding recruits who have completed basic training, veteran paratroopers and serving soldiers in other regiments. Prospective recruits to the Jordanian 101st Special Forces must be East Bank desert bedouins with a proven record of loyalty to King Hussein and close tribal links to the ruling Hashemite royal family. In Oman, volunteers from the Airborne Regiment can try to join the Independent Reconnaissance Regiment, but only Dhofaris (inhabitants of Dhofar Province, in the west of the country) are accepted (officers in elite Omani infantry battalions are still mainly ex-British and Rhodesian SAS). Such selectivity, though ensuring loyalty, tends to reduce overall effectiveness because it means the unit has to draw its members from a relatively small manpower pool.

At the first level of comparison, therefore, it can be seen that many potential SAS soldiers are not as highly qualified as recruits to other units, particularly in America and the Far East

An SAS soldier must be a man who can become a team player

Individuals are the building blocks upon which an elite unit is formed, but many who have the relevant entry qualifications to volunteer, and who put themselves forward for selection, fail the initial selection courses (failure rates can be as high as 90 per cent). This is because they do not have the personal qualities required to become effective members of a special forces team. But what are these qualities, and how do SAS recruitment officers go about finding them?

In a recent memorandum, the UK Director of Special Forces listed the individual qualities looked for in potential recruits to 22 SAS Regiment. These were motivation and determination, initiative, self-discipline, compatibility for small-group, long-term, isolated operations, an aptitude to assimilate a wide range of skills, and the ability to think laterally. The Australian and New Zealand SAS look for similar mental and physical qualities, though the Australians tend to

look for recruits with the mental ability that will allow them to develop these qualities.

An SAS soldier must be a man who can become a team player, who can learn a variety of skills, and who has a level of fitness that is far above that of personnel in conventional units. Naturally, many of the qualities looked for in SAS recruits are also required for other elite units. Endurance and stamina are universal qualities, as are initiative and intelligence. Nevertheless, it is the SAS soldier's ability to be a multi-skilled performer who can operate in a small group (usually a four-man team) for long periods, often behind enemy lines, and undertake a wide variety of military tasks, that makes him special among the elite forces brotherhood.

SAS Selection Training lasts for one month and is held at Hereford

No one would deny that British Paras and Royal Marines, French Foreign Legionnaires, Israeli Paras and German Mountain Troops are all highly motivated, but they are not expected to fulfil the variety of missions undertaken by SAS soldiers. Prospective SAS soldiers must therefore possess the potential to assimilate even more skills than many of their foreign counterparts.

There are only two other elite organisations that look for the same range of qualities in recruits as the SAS: the US Green Berets and SEALs. The Green Berets look for intelligent men with high levels of endurance, men who are highly-motivated team players with good military records, and who have a very high standard of basic infantry skills. The SEALs look for stamina, motivation, initiative, intelligence and manual dexterity, together with high aptitude for technical matters, particularly engineering.

What about the actual selection courses themselves – our second level of comparison. How do they measure up?

The initial training course a candidate must negotiate on his way to being awarded the famed winged dagger badge is Selection Training. The course lasts for one month and is

Above: Candidates on the Green Beret Q Course. The US Special Forces, in particular, look for endurance and intelligence in recruits.

run twice a year, in the summer and in the winter. Run from the Regiment's headquarters at Stirling Lines, Hereford, it is divided into a three-week build-up period and Test Week, which is the culmination of Selection. The course itself, which is administered by Training Wing, consists of a series of road runs which increase in length over the first week, followed by a set of testing marches over the Black Mountains and Brecon Beacons of South Wales. Each man is given a bergen, compass and map (the weight carried is 18kg plus personal weapon). He is then given a grid reference for

the first rendezvous. When he reaches it he is given the grid reference for the next rendezvous, and so on. All the time he is being watched and assessed by the training staff, who will be keeping an eye out to see if he fails to display the requisite personal qualities.

The terrain he has to traverse is physically draining because it is extremely hilly and subject to frequent and erratic weather changes. If it rains his bergen will absorb moisture and get heavier, if he gets lost he will have to jog to keep within the time set for the exercise. At rendezvous points he may be asked to field-strip a foreign weapon, or answer questions concerning a landmark he has passed some time back. His reactions and answers will be carefully monitored at all times to ascertain whether he

Above: SEAL recruits are put through their paces at the Naval Amphibious School. The BUDS course rivals SAS Selection in intensity.

has the qualities and attributes required to make an SAS soldier.

The candidates have very little time for themselves, and very little time for their bodies and minds to recuperate. For example, each day begins at around 0400 hours and ends at 2230 hours or later, when a briefing is held for the next day's exercise. The result is cumulative mental and physical tiredness, while the course itself gets both more physically and more mentally demanding as it progresses. This is intentional, and ensures only the best get through.

As the Director of Special Forces puts it: 'There is no question that the course is hard and demands total commitment from the individual if he is to be successful, but the rewards in terms of personal achievement and job satisfaction are high. At the outset individual motivation is the key.' For many the course is all the harder because each man is on his own. The Director of Special Forces again: 'There is neither active encouragement nor discouragement and the attitude of the Instructors/Training Staff remains neutral. Individuals may voluntarily withdraw themselves from the course at any time.' With no mates or instructors to urge encouragement many men do drop out and are returned to their parent unit ('RTU'd' in British Army slang).

The climax of Test Week is the 64km Endurance March in South Wales

This 'neutrality' on the part of the training staff marks the first major difference between the SAS and many other elite units around the world. The SAS soldier is an individual who can work within a team. Other units, such as the French Foreign Legion and British Paras, emphasise the unit rather than the individual. The Spanish Legion, for example, discourages initiative altogether and requires a total commitment to the Legion and its traditions. Hand in hand with this ethos goes an iron-hard discipline which is more akin to the nineteenth century than the twenty-first.

The culmination of SAS Selection is Test Week, and the climax of that is the 64km Endurance March over the Brecon Beacons, nicknamed 'Long Drag' or 'Fan Dance'. Each man carries 25kg plus personal weapon, and must complete the course within 20 hours, regardless of the weather. For many, 'Long Drag' is the final straw. On Selection Training at the beginning of 1992, for example, out of the 149 men who started, 61 failed the pass times for marches, 59 voluntarily withdrew, six dropped out injured and another eight were 'binned' by the instructors. Only 15 were judged suitable to attempt the next phase of SAS training.

At this stage of SAS training the emphasis is very much on physical endurance, allied to mental determination. The instructors are looking for men who can keep going and think straight when their bodies are exhausted. In this, SAS Selection differs little from that of other elite units around the world. The Australian SAS, for example, has an endurance course codenamed 'Happy Wanderer' after the Regimental marching song. The culmination of the course is a five-day endurance march that takes the recruits over five mountain-top checkpoints. Each man carries a 50kg bergen, which alters his centre of gravity and makes it even more difficult to climb the steep mountain sides (the bergens have a habit of snaring themselves on the dense mountain scrub, and each time they are lifted off they feel that bit heavier when they are put back on again).

The philosophy behind the course is explained by an Australian SAS training wing major thus (note how similar it is to the British SAS): 'Here the man with the self-discipline, initiative and strength of character to keep going, when the going gets really tough, will succeed. He must prove he can make rational decisions and maintain his morale without a companion to encourage him or act as a prop.'

The Ranger Indoctrination Program is designed to 'weed out the quitters'

Pushing candidates to their physical and mental limits is the objective of the US Army Ranger Indoctrination Program, conducted at Fort Benning. This is a tough three-week course designed to 'weed out the quitters'. The students are tested in a wide variety of military skills, including two days of static-line parachuting from CH-47 Chinook twin-rotor helicopters using MC1-B steerable parachutes. All newly assigned men who are not parachute-trained are first sent on the three-week Airborne Course, also held at Fort Benning; the few failures are sent to other non-airborne units. The Program also teaches basic infantry skills, combat skills and airmobile techniques (usually abseiling to the ground from a helicopter). The students then practise ambush techniques, reconnaissance, navigation drills and abseiling down cliffs by day and night.

The course ends with a series of physical tests, timed runs, marches carrying full kit (including a 19.3km march to be completed in three hours) and the Ranger Water Survival Test (swimming with kit). Between 40 and 50 per cent fail the course and are sent to other units. The major difference between this course and SAS Selection is that the men receive encouragement from the instructors and team mates. Because of this, the Ranger course must be considered easier than Selection.

Similarly hard is the SEALs' BUDS training programme. This 23-week course is run at the SEAL Training Department of the Naval Amphibious School in Virginia, and weeks 1-5 are akin to SAS Selection Training. A large part of the first four weeks for the 500-700 volunteers are spent on physical training, team games and water sports. If this sounds easy it is not: every element of training is competitive, as the teams race against the clock and each other. However, it must once again be regarded as easier than

SAS Selection, if only because team mates urge each other on.

Of these first four weeks, the first two are basically a warm-up period devoted to purely physical activity, but the next two are spent learning how to handle small boats, conduct beach reconnaissance and assimilate long-range land patrol skills. Proficiency in these skills is achieved through many live-firing exercises, and the students are under constant pressure to improve accuracy, timing and teamwork.

Week five of the BUDS programme is nicknamed 'Hell Week'. This is when the physical and mental endurance of each student are tested to the limit, and on little food or sleep. By this stage around half the students will have left the course, either by being terminated by the instructors or ringing a brass bell three times to

Below: A Spetsnaz recruit negotiates an obstacle course. Russia's fighting elite proved their physical stamina in Afghanistan.

Above: Galil-armed Israeli Paras on the assault course. Israel's airborne elite are the battle-hardened shield of the Jewish state.

signal their voluntary withdrawal. Weeks 6-23 of the BUDS course is comparable to SAS Continuation Training and will dealt with below.

Prospective recruits to the US Special Forces arrive at the John F. Kennedy Special Warfare Center and School at Fort Bragg, North Carolina, to face a gruelling three-week pre-selection test known as Special Forces Assessment and Selection (SFAS). Designed as a cost-cutting measure, whereby candidates who may otherwise have dropped out of Special Forces selection after consuming valuable time and money are sifted out before the course starts, it involves long-distance runs, bergen marches and confidence and obstacle courses. Like SAS Selection it is tough: around half the average class of 300 fail SFAS.

Those who pass win a place on the Special Forces Qualification Course (Q Course), which is more academic in content than SAS Selection. Phase I of the course, for example, lasts five

weeks and covers patrolling, close combat, airborne insertion, and survival and land navigation. Survival, camouflage and concealment, rope work, abseiling, and navigation are taught by the Land Navigation and General Subjects Committees; the art of patrolling within the 12-man A-Team (the Green Beret operational unit) is taught by the Patrolling Committee.

This training is tested over 12 consecutive nights, when the students are asked to navigate from one point to another in the Uwharrie National Forest. All the time they are watched to see if they have absorbed what they have been taught and how well they maintain self-reliance and discipline. Upon the successful completion of Phase I the Green Beret is awarded. As with the SAS, aspiring Green Berets are not subjected to any external pressures: self-motivation is the key to whether they pass or fail.

The basic training of other elite units varies considerably from that of the SAS, SEALs and Green Berets, and must be considered inferior. The Spanish Legion, for example, has a six-month basic training course that consists mainly of drill and fitness training, weapons drills and

platoon field drills. Accompanying this is a harsh regime that allows NCOs to physically assault their charges and demands total subservience to the Legion. The result is brutalised soldiers who have almost zero initiative.

The French Foreign Legion did have an unsavoury reputation for brutality, but physical abuse of recruits has now been greatly reduced. The first month of basic training is still very physically tough, though, with recruits expected to be able to complete a 60km march with full military load over two days at the end of the fourth week. The military training during this period focuses on weapons maintenance, uniform appearance, individual load-carrying and drilling. Initiative is discouraged, and, unlike SAS training, is accompanied by encouragement and often virulent abuse from the instructors throughout the course.

Many members of the British Parachute Regiment, a unit famed for its tenacity in battle, go on to wear the winged dagger badge, but the selection training in the Paras differs in emphasis from that undertaken in the SAS. The psychology behind the training is to foster a team spirit, whereby each team member will want to succeed not only for himself, but also in order not to let down his mates. Such identification with the team also gives recruits an excellent incentive to do well, since if a man is back-squadded it will mean him leaving his mates in the section and joining another squad, where he will be an outsider – this he will want to avoid.

The first four gruelling weeks of basic training are spent in fitness training, competitive sports, runs (without boots), weapons skills, drill and kit inspections. Until week four the recruits have an entitlement to 'discharge by right', whereby they can quit the course of their own volition (up to 30 per cent of volunteers can be lost in this way). After that they either progress to the next stage of training or else they are back-squadded to begin the course all over again.

Above: Australian SAS recruits go through hell during Selection. If they make it they will be among the best elite soldiers on earth.

At the end of the second level of comparison, it can be seen that the SAS, SEALs and Green Berets lead the way, though the emphasis is still mainly on physical fitness and mental endurance. The third level of comparison, post-selection training, sees the gap widen between the SAS, SEALs and Green Berets and other units.

Post-selection training may mean embarking on another course, or going on to the second stage of the selection course. Whichever it is, the pressure on individuals increases. The physical demands remain, but recruits are now also expected to assimilate a wide variety of military skills. And all the time the threat of being 'binned' hangs over them like the Sword of Damocles.

Selection Training is the first hurdle potential SAS recruits have to surmount. The second hurdle, Continuation Training, is also difficult, but those candidates who are left are judged to have the qualities to become SAS soldiers, and the course is less to do with weeding out the unfit than with imparting SAS skills. Recruits can still be RTU'd and they are

still being tested, but by this stage they are also being taught.

Continuation lasts 14 weeks, during which time the students are taught basic SAS skills that enable them to become effective members of a four-man patrol (the smallest SAS operational unit, which combines optimum mobility with maximum firepower). The recruits are taught SAS standard operating procedures (SOPs) and receive instruction in all the Regiment's patrol skills: signalling, field medicine, demolitions and languages. After Continuation comes Jungle Training and static-line parachuting, which must be considered as being part of SAS post-selection training.

The four-man patrol is a self-contained unit, and comprising soldiers with the above combination of skills can operate at its maximum efficiency. Communications skills ensure that the patrol is able to keep in touch with other

units and the high command. Language skills are imperative for cultivating links between a patrol and indigenous peoples should the need arise. Indeed languages are crucial to the SAS's 'hearts and minds' policy (in Malaya, for example, SAS troopers spoke the language of the jungle Aborigines). Demolition skills are essential for sabotage operations, and medicine is not only useful for the treatment of patrol members, but can also be used to treat indigenous peoples and therefore aid 'hearts and minds' missions.

In patrol tactics, each patrol member is assigned his own specific role. The lead scout will cover the area to the front of the patrol between 10 o'clock and two o'clock. The man behind him, usually the patrol commander, covers the arc between six o'clock and 10 o'clock or two o'clock to six o'clock, while another man covers the arc opposite. The 'Tailend Charlie' is responsible for covering the rear of the patrol.

Continuation Training is conducted at a frenetic pace, with each man being expected not to learn simply the basics of any subject, but to achieve a degree of proficiency in it as well. For example, each man is expected to be able to transmit and receive Morse code at a minimum of eight words a minute.

Recruits are also instructed in basic fieldcraft – target reconnaissance, weapons

exercise even those who have successfully evaded their 'foes' have to surrender and then be subjected to a Resistance-to-Interrogation exercise. The men are put under both mental and physical stress, all of which iş designed to force them to reveal more information to their interrogators than the 'Big Four': number, rank, name and date of birth. Those who crack have failed Continuation and are sent back to their units forthwith.

Officers' Week is a test that consists of exercises and written projects

Following the successful completion of Continuation Training, all candidates are then sent on a jungle training course (4-6 weeks in the Far East, usually Brunei), where they learn all aspects of jungle survival and operations (the SAS has a 40-year association with the jungle, having fought successful jungle campaigns in both Malaya and Borneo). The course culminates in a final exercise which all the students must pass. They are split into four-man patrols and given a specific task which will test all the skills they have learned over the preceding weeks. Even at this late stage a man can fail, a cruel blow but one that is necessary to maintain the Regiment's high standards.

Officers' Week falls directly after Jungle Training. For officers who wish to join the SAS (and who have passed Selection and Continuation), this is a critical test that consists of exercises, appreciations and written projects, all designed to determine whether a candidate can think clearly and logically under stress (students average 15 hours of sleep over five days). Assessments are made by a combination of SAS and SBS personnel, and can often involve lower ranks deriding the plans of officers, which can be particularly galling. The final decision rests with the commanding officers of the SAS and SBS, and the Director of Special Forces.

The qualities looked for in SAS officers are: motivation and commitment, character and

training, ground control of artillery and aircraft fire – and they are subjected to a host of initiative tests. In addition, each course ends with a test that all must pass. The threat of being RTU'd never goes away, and is an additional pressure on the men.

Continuation ends with a Combat and Survival phase (three weeks on Exmoor), where the students learn every aspect of living in hostile environments: building shelters, finding food and water, laying traps and lighting fires. Combat and Survival ends with an Escape and Evasion exercise, during which the prospective SAS troopers have to evade the 'enemy' (usually a local infantry battalion). At the end of the integrity, logical and lateral thought, organisational ability, adaptability, decisiveness, intelligence, common sense, and overall confidence.

The week starts with an initial exercise where each candidate introduces himself to the audience and talks about his background and ambitions. There then follows a series of problematical exercises, during which the students are required to present their deductions and solutions and answer questions. In addition, candidates are given a written project each day and a practical task each night.

At the end of the course they are awarded their 'Sabre' wings

All candidates are subjected to close scrutiny, and they may be ridiculed if they do not come up to scratch. If they are, the reactions of students (who will not be used to lower ranks treating them in this manner) will be carefully noted by the examiners. Many fail, not because they are not good officers, far from it, but because they do not have that unique blend of unassuming professionalism, decisiveness, energy and humour found in SAS officers.

The final hurdle for both officers and men is the static-line parachute course, which lasts four weeks and is held at the Parachute Training School at RAF Brize Norton, Oxfordshire. Each man makes a total of eight jumps, including one at night and one operational descent (those who are already parachute-trained do not take the course). At the end of the course they are awarded their 'Sabre' wings and then return to Stirling Lines, where they are 'badged' SAS.

How do other units' post-selection courses compare? Post-selection training in the Australian SAS has similar components to that of its British counterpart. Selection is followed by an SAS Patrol Course, which teaches individual patrolling skills, and then by a static-line parachute course. At this point the soldier is posted to the Regiment and enters the Reinforcement Training Cycle to learn basic demolitions, weapons handling and survival skills. Then comes the Regimental Signaller's Course, conducted by the staff of 152 Signal Squadron. At the end of the course each student

must be able to send Morse code at a speed of 10 words per minute (which is higher than the British SAS). Students then receive instruction in combat medicine by attached staff from the Army School of Health.

On the successful completion of all these courses, the 'Reinforcements' receive training in the basic skill of the troop to which they will be posted: Water Operations Troop, Freefall Troop or the Vehicle Mounted Troop.

The second phase of training for US elite units is similar to that undertaken by the SAS, with the recruits being instructed in operational techniques. The emphasis is on honing the intellect rather than physical stamina, and is in many ways tougher than SAS Continuation. Phase II of the Green Berets' Q Course, for example, is designed to teach individual specialities and turn the students themselves into teachers. Candidates choose their own speciality (though there may be coercion on the part of instructors to make up numbers in some undersubscribed areas). The course normally lasts five weeks, but those who elect to specialise in medicine have to do a further eight weeks.

Medical specialists spend 13 weeks at the Academy of Health Sciences

Those who choose to become weapons specialists receive instruction in all aspects of light and heavy weaponry (light weapons include handguns, rifles, machine guns, submachine guns and grenade launchers; heavy weapons comprise mortars, rocket launchers, and anti-tank and anti-aircraft missile launchers). Up to 60 foreign and obsolete weapons are also studied because they are likely to end up in the hands of guerrilla units, and therefore students may eventually have to train the personnel of insurgency groups in their use.

The explosives and demolitions speciality covers manufactured and home-made explosives, the construction and demolition of structures and engineer reconnaissance. Radio specialists focus on the use and repair of special forces radios covering the FM, UHF and satellite communications (SATCOM) bands. Tuition also covers aerial construction, burst-

message transmission, frequency-hopping devices, cryptographic systems, counter-electronic intelligence (ELINT) and radio security.

Medical specialists spend 13 weeks at the US Army's Academy of Health Sciences at Fort Sam Houston, Texas, where they learn about war surgery, anaesthesia, intravenous fluids, preventive medicine, dangerous animal bites, dental surgery, cardiopulmonary resuscitation, primitive resuscitation, mental illness, and blast and temperature injuries. This is followed by six weeks spent administering casualty and emergency care at various Army hospitals and six weeks of patient care. They also receive instruction in gynaecology and veterinary science – useful skills for winning the affections of locals during counter-insurgency operations.

Phase III of the Q Course consists of four weeks of unconventional warfare training and mission planning followed by a two-week exercise, in which all the classroom work is brought together and tested. Students are

Above: American Rangers on exercise. These elite infantrymen of the US Army are all parachute-qualified.

dropped into the woodlands and swamps of the Uwharrie National Forest as part of Exercise 'Robin Sage'. In this simulated 'hostile nation' students have to rendezvous with 'friendly natives' drawn from families that live in the area. The students have to demonstrate that they can teach the locals weapons skills and organise them into guerrilla units. While this is happening, hunter-killer teams from the 82nd Airborne Division search for the 'partisans' and their Green Beret instructors. In the final phase of the exercise, the prospective Green Berets lead their guerrilla units on ambushes and raids against the 'aggressor force'.

There is an additional hazard for the students: some of the locals have natural sympathies for the 82nd Airborne, and so the students must be on their guard to ensure they do not fall into the wrong hands (which would jeopardise their chances of selection for the Special Forces – something they will obviously want to avoid). After successfully completing all three phases of training, a student is then Special Forces Flash qualified.

The second part of Ranger training consists of 8-12 months learning small unit tactics, patrolling techniques and combat skills. More specialised training is to be found on the Ranger Course, which is compulsory for NCO and officer command positions within the 75th Ranger Regiment. The course is also open to Army, Navy and Air Force special forces; other regular Army and Army Reserve National Guard personnel; college officer cadets and West Point cadets; Navy and Air Force personnel; and guest allied soldiers.

Specialist training on the SEALs' BUDS course begins in week six

Before they take the Ranger Course, all candidates are sent on the four-week Pre-Ranger Program that prepares them for the course by reviewing basic skills and honing their physical fitness. The Ranger Course itself lasts for 65 days and aims to teach combat and leadership skills in a realistic environment. The students are kept under relentless pressure, with 'impossible' time limits within which to accomplish missions, and food and sleep deprivation.

Reconnaissance patrol work is undertaken in a number of demanding environments. Throughout the course, all students are required to plan and lead increasingly difficult patrols. To make matters worse, there is an ever-present professional aggressor force that acts as the enemy.

Specialist training on the SEALs' BUDS course begins in week six, when the students receive instruction in diving skills. At San Clemente Island they are taught underwater and land demolitions, and complete a series of long swims, culminating in an 8km marathon. The students are also introduced to the vehicles that are used to transport SEAL teams close to their target, such as the Ethan Allen class submarines *Thomas A. Edison* and *John Marshall*. Each one can carry pods containing Swimmer Delivery Vehicles (SDVs) that can convey the teams through treacherous tides and currents to the enemy coast.

Tuition goes on to cover underwater communications using a UTEL microphone and the sabotage of enemy shipping with limpet mines, demolition charges and long-range Mark 37 torpedoes, which can be fired from SDVs such as the EX-IX. Weeks 6-23 of SEAL training end with several small-boat and swimming exercises under simulated wartime conditions. Then there is instruction in specialised underwater warfare techniques and a static-line parachute course. Trainees learn how to make 'wet' drops into the sea (SEAL team members also learn HALO and HAHO parachuting after they qualify, because missions may take them inland and far from the coast). The going is tough. By the end of BUDS, 55 per cent of volunteers have failed and left the course.

Meanwhile, the second phase programmes in the selection process for west European elite units (excluding the SAS) tend not to be as intensive as those of the Green Berets and SEALs. Whereas in the initial phase of selection they were being tested purely on their levels of mental and physical endurance, at this stage of

Below: Members of South Korea's 'Capital Command' practise their martial arts in a display of controlled aggression.

their training the recruits are being prepared for their unit's chosen role, and the training they receive reflects this. Military skills are taught; nevertheless there is still great emphasis on physical stamina.

Weeks 5-12 of basic training for the British Parachute Regiment, for example, still emphasise physical endurance, aggression and the ability to work as part of a team. A member of 3 Para put it succinctly: 'Our troops are more aggressive than any other troops anyway, and it all boils down to the training and the type of guy needed to pass that training. We find that the aggression amongst our blokes is very high: they are very aggressive.' This aggression is fostered through a series of brutal test exercises which each man must pass in order to get through the course.

The emphasis of the second phase of basic training is physical

Week 12 signals the start of P Company, a three-week period in which the prospective Paras prepare themselves for Test Week, or Pre-Parachute Selection. As well as the usual physical hurdles, there is the Trainasium, which consists of walkways 7m off the ground and shuffle bars 15m off the ground. Here they test to see if a man has what it takes to jump out of an aircraft – between three and 10 per cent fail outright. The Stretcher Race lasts for one hour and 20 minutes. This is run over a 12km course by teams bearing a 75kg steel stretcher on which each member is carried in turn. A Para instructor explains: 'At the end of the day, when we have got a good team spirit going, then because of the responsibility that a man feels for the others on his team, he will not let them down. P Company brings that out of them, because no one can hide. It is a course that you can't hide on, and we get the right type of person at the end of it: we get a reliable man on the battlefield.'

Although the famous Parachute Regiment red beret is awarded after the successful completion of Pre-Selection, training is not over yet. Next the recruits have to win their wings. This involves a 20-day parachute course at RAF Brize Norton. Compared with what has gone before, this is something akin to a rest cure.

As in the Paras, the emphasis of the second phase of basic training for the Royal Marines is still physical. Some training is specifically Marine-oriented – seamanship, amphibious operations, rapid deployment from vehicles, mock cliff assaults. But there is also much endurance work: 10 and 14.5km speed marches, long marches over Dartmoor, endurance marches and – the culmination of the course – a 48km march across Dartmoor in full kit that must be completed within eight hours. When this has been successfully completed the students are awarded the coveted green berets.

Training for the Belgian Para-Commandos is necessarily limited because most trainees are conscripts who serve for only one year. Therefore, Phase 2 (operational training) and Phase 3 (a parachute course), last only one month each. Nevertheless, the unit is still able to more than fulfil its primary role: the reinforcement of the Belgian 1st Corps in the Northern Army Group.

The Israeli Parachute Corps turns out highly motivated soldiers

The French Foreign Legion's second and third months of basic training are devoted to weapons skills, drills, forced marches, climbing, abseiling and advanced field craft. Physical endurance is still a major requirement: for example, in the 12th week students have to complete a 200km mountain march in full kit in four days.

Some of the other elite units around the world have very intensive post-selection training programmes. South Korea's 'Capital Command', for example, has adopted many of the training methods used by its ally the United States. Basic training is followed by an intensive two-month Ranger Course, which teaches all aspects of elite reconnaissance work and specialist skills (communications, support weapons, medicine and demolitions). In addition, each student is expected to devote at least five hours a day to martial arts training to develop his endurance and self-discipline.

The Israeli Parachute Corps is another unit that turns out highly motivated soldiers. The five-month Israeli Commando Course teaches all aspects of infantry assault procedures – helicopter and armoured fighting vehicle deployment, night fighting, fighting in urban areas and close-quarter battle skills – as well as the speciality of the Paras: taking and holding strongpoints. The subsequent one-month parachute course is easier than its British equivalent, and failure rates are quite low.

Countries that have been influenced by both the United States and the Soviet Union tend to have a confusing mixture of Western and Warsaw Pact military doctrine, and this is reflected in their special forces training programmes. The Egyptian Commandos, for example, are trained to seize strategic points behind enemy lines (a Spetsnaz doctrine), but they are also trained as shock light infantry (which is the role of the French Foreign Legion and Belgian Para-Commandos, for example). These conflicts would seem to negate the unit's overall effectiveness.

Soldiers have to learn a diversity of skills to be members of 22 SAS

Phase 2 of the training for Oman's Independent Reconnaissance Regiment is based on SAS Continuation Training, while Phase 3 is a period of operational deployment with the Reconnaissance Regiment and involves patrolling the southwestern border of Oman. Jordan's 101st Special Forces are trained as commando and ranger elite infantry, and the six-month Phase II of their basic training emphasises this, with long-range reconnaissance work, desert survival and urban combat training. Though there is a parachute course (3-4 weeks), Jordan's lack of dedicated transport aircraft brings into question the usefulness of having para-trained special forces.

Thailand's Special Forces model their organisation and training on their American counterparts. After general training each student concentrates on his own specialisation: medicine, demolitions, communications or weapons skills. Thai weapon skills training places particular emphasis on communist weapons, such as those in the hands of Cambodian and Laotian forces and the many insurgent groups in the area, especially in the Golden Triangle.

How does SAS post-selection training compare to that of other elite units? It would be wrong to state that SAS recruits at this stage of their training are further advanced than other special forces personnel. Indeed, US Green Beret and SEAL recruits could claim to be more highly trained at this stage of their careers, as also could the South Koreans. It is at the next

Above: Royal Marine recruits negotiate ice-cold water during training. Winning the green beret is an arduous task for the young volunteers.

level of training, advanced training, that SAS recruits begin to pull ahead when compared with their rivals. This advanced training forms the fourth level of comparison.

Newly 'badged' Special Air Service soldiers serve a probationary period of 12 months. During this time they are expected to learn a patrol skill (medicine, demolitions, communications or languages) as well as the particular skills of the troop to which they have been assigned. There are four troops in an SAS Sabre squadron, each one of which has its own area of expertise: Mountain Troop, Boat Troop, Mobility Troop and Air Troop.

An SAS soldier will invariably pick up a second, even a third, patrol skill as he spends more time with the Regiment, and training at all levels and in all skills is a continuous process for every SAS trooper. In this sense there is no such thing as a fully trained SAS soldier.

In addition to patrol and troop skills, SAS squadrons are rotated through Counter Revolutionary Warfare (CRW) training at Hereford. The Regiment's CRW Wing at Hereford teaches all aspects of counter-terrorism, including hostage-rescue, and at any one time there is a squadron on 24-hour standby for counter-terrorist and hostage-rescue operations.

The SEALs put their men through rigorous advanced training

The Australian SAS also provides advanced training, which covers shooting, fieldcraft, land and astro-navigation, small unit tactics, troop specialist skills and operational procedures.

The US Green Berets have advanced training systems that match those of the SAS in intensity and scope. Green Beret recruits undertake region orientation – i.e. learning the customs, culture and languages of the region allotted to the Special Forces Group to which they are assigned. Students also undertake weather, climate and terrain training. Advanced training at Fort Bragg includes a snipers' course, HALO and HAHO parachute courses (see By Air Chapter), underwater swimming and intelligence work.

The SEALs, too, put their men through rigorous advanced training. On the post-selection training course at the Special Warfare Center and School, Fort Bragg, for example, candidates are taught most of the subjects found on the Special Forces selection course. As in the SAS, SEAL training is never complete, and this is borne out by the fact that 30 per cent of a man's subsequent career is spent on further courses and training, such as deep reconnaissance, SDV driver courses, operating mini submarines, and bomb and mine disposal. Such training creates the elite of elite soldiers.

Advanced training within west European elite units usually entails recruits joining a specialist part of the parent organisation. The Parachute Regiment, for example, has the Pathfinder Platoon, while the Mountain and Arctic Warfare Cadre (M&AWC) and SBS are part of the Royal Marines. The Royal Netherlands Marine Corps has 7 Netherlands SBS, Whiskey Company and the Marine Close Combat Unit, and the Belgian Para-Commandos has a Long Range Reconnaissance Patrol Company.

An elite within the French Foreign Legion is the 2e *Régiment Etranger de Parachutistes* (2e REP), and Legionnaires wishing to join this parachute unit must pass a para-commando course. Only 30 per cent succeed. There is another section within the Foreign Legion – another elite within an elite – called the Reconnaissance and Deep Action Commandos Platoon. The selection process for this unit is still classified, but it is thought to be extremely tough.

Since the beginning of 1994, Royal Marines wishing to join the SBS have had to pass SAS Selection Training (see above). Specialist training within the SBS is divided into aptitude testing and trade training, to prepare men for covert waterborne operations. Training includes beach survey and photography, endurance canoeing and swimming exercises, small boat training, parachute descents at sea, coastal and underwater navigation, and astro-navigation.

The elite within an elite in the Paras is the Pathfinder Platoon

The M&AWC course lasts 16 months and covers all aspects of mountain and arctic warfare. The course is more or less akin to SAS Continuation Training in layout and aim. For example, after spending the entire winter in Norway undergoing arctic warfare training, the students complete a Pathfinder Course in the Ben Nevis area of Scotland, followed by a static-line parachuting course at RAF Brize Norton. The final months of the course are spent in the Lake District, Cumbria, learning and teaching alpine techniques, which are then tested on Exercise 'Ice Flip' in Switzerland. The selection

process on the course is by continuous assessment and takes account of both classroom tests and field work.

The elite within an elite in The Parachute Regiment is the Pathfinder Platoon, whose members are tasked with 'lighting up the dropping zones' and performing deep-penetration raids and patrols. It numbers only 30 men and, unsurprisingly, the competition for membership is intense.

The three-week selection course is designed to select those men who can offer a bit more than the usual professional Para skills. Navigation and endurance walks are combined with tactical exercises and assault courses, culminating in the volunteers 'tabbing' 50km across the Welsh mountains or the wilds of Dartmoor's North Moor, carrying an equipment load of in excess of 25kg. The whole selection process is very tough, and as a result the pass rate is less than 10 per cent.

The specialist unit within the Spanish Legion is the *Bandera Especiales de la Legion*

Above: A Spanish Legionnaire. There are no entry requirements for Spain's elite. Recruits tend to be in their early 20s.

(BOEL), which is organised into special operations platoons. The initial selection period lasts six months, during which time the students are subjected to physical and mental tests. In the Resistance-to-Interrogation phase they must reveal nothing, not even their names. Although the pass rate for the course is high, the accompanying injury and fatality rates are also high.

Units that have conscripts in their ranks face a problem when it comes to forming specialist units: their only pool of recruits consists of volunteers who are on longer engagements. However, many of these men also form the backbone of the unit's support cadres, such as training and logistics groups. This is certainly the case in the Belgian Para-Commandos, where volunteers carry out specialised battalion tasks – signals, combat medicine, intelligence and transport – while also bearing the brunt of

Above: A Spanish Legionnaire under fire on the assault course. The Legion's training is unimaginative and brutal.

support tasks. This means that not many men can be spared for specialist combat units, a major weakness. The specialist unit with the Para-Commandos, the Long Range Reconnaissance Patrol Company, is tasked with collecting intelligence and carrying out raids behind enemy lines, though its strength is only around 50 men (out of a regimental strength of 1000). Volunteers for this unit face a selection course similar to that of the British SAS.

The South Korean 'Capital Command' has some of the most highly trained special forces units in the world, and they stand comparison with other elite units, the British SAS included, but they are necessarily orientated towards the specific requirement of deterring and defeating North Korean aggression.

The specialised units with the Korean 'Capital Command' are the three Long Range Reconnaissance (LRR) Companies (Airborne), the two professional Special Warfare Command Brigades and the Surveillance/Reconnaissance

Battalions. They are all trained to work behind North Korean lines, and the Special Warfare Command brigades are also tasked with training South Korean paramilitary forces and leading them on guerrilla operations should areas of South Korea be overrun by North Korean forces in a future conflict.

The elite sayeret units of the Israeli forces are made up of high-calibre volunteers who have already proved their worth. Sayeret Golani, for example, will not take a man on its six-month training course unless he already has combat experience.

Since an individual's training for the British SAS never really ends, it is difficult to make an assessment of how good the unit is in comparison with other elite organisations. Nevertheless, it is this unending training that sets the SAS apart and makes it the bench mark by which other special forces are measured.

Although the personnel of other elite units undergo continuous training, it is the scope and diversity of the SAS's training that makes its soldiers different from the rest. US Green Berets, for example, are primarily trainers (they trained Arab forces during the 1991 Gulf War, for example), and in this they are excellent. But the Regiment's achievement in Oman during the 1970s, when they successfully trained Arab irregular units to fight communist guerrillas, convincingly demonstrates that Hereford's soldiers can also fulfil this role.

The collapse of communism in the Soviet Union and the other countries of the former Warsaw Pact has left some elite groups in doubt about their future roles. The Spanish Legion is putting off a decision by continuing to train for a NATO versus Warsaw Pact conflict, even though it is not combat-ready, has no air assets, artillery or heavy armour. Even The Parachute Regiment has no fixed role: it is unlikely that many 'Out of Area' operations will be launched in the immediate future, and the likelihood of the Paras having to make a wartime static-line jump appears more remote than ever before.

The Australian and New Zealand SAS, because of the geography of their respective countries, emphasise seaborne insertion operations, and the New Zealanders are in reality primarily concerned with counter-terrorism (New Zealand has no natural enemies and is far away from other countries: so why should it train for a war that will never break out?).

Are there any shortcomings in Special Air Service training?

Are there any shortcomings in SAS training? In truth it is difficult to find anything wrong with a system that produces soldiers who are at home fighting in the humid jungles of the Far East (Malaya 1948-60, Borneo 1963-66), the searing heat of the Arabian desert (Oman 1958-59, 1970-76, the Gulf 1990-91) and the frozen wastes of the South Atlantic (1982), and who can perform tasks as diverse as operating behind enemy lines (Falklands War), conducting raids and ambushes (North Africa 1941-43, Pebble Island 1982), carrying out 'hearts and minds' policies, and undertaking counter-terrorist duties (Northern Ireland 1969-present, Princes Gate 1980). However, one current problem with regard to the SAS is that it is a victim of its own success – i.e. it is so much in demand that its resources are overstretched. This could have

serious ramifications with regard to deployments and morale in the future.

There are other units that have very few deficiencies. The US Navy SEALs are trained to a high degree of excellence. The Royal Thai Special Forces are the most professional force in Southeast Asia, and they have been responsible for helping the Thai Army defeat two communist insurgencies inside Thailand, as well as successfully assisting US forces during the Vietnam War. The only shortcoming of South Korea's 'Capital Command' is its relatively small size compared to North Korea's special forces.

The US Navy SEALs are trained to a high degree of excellence

The excellence of SAS soldiers and their high reputation throughout the world have led to great demands on their time and manpower resources. In addition to being deployed throughout the world and in readiness for new assignments at short notice, they are also committed to providing advisers in many regions. At the time of writing, SAS men are in Northern Ireland, Belize, Brunei, the United States and many parts of the Middle East.

How can one assess excellence? It is a difficult question, but one that perhaps can be answered by taking a look at the numbers of men who volunteer for the SAS each year and how many actually end up wearing the beige beret and winged dagger badge. Around 300 men put themselves forward for Selection Training each year. Between 20 and 30 win the famed winged dagger badge, though in some years it is less. Other units, such as the SEALs and Green Berets, also have high failure rates, though not as high as that of the British SAS. Even the Australian and New Zealand SAS pass more men in an average year.

For the SAS training staff at Stirling Lines at Hereford this failure rate is perfectly acceptable, even desirable. For those who put themselves forward for Selection Training, however, it is an indication of the daunting task they face, and is perhaps an indication that the British Special Air Service is the hardest unit in the world to become a member of.

WEAPONS SKILLS

The ability to aim and shoot a weapon competently is a basic military skill. For elite soldiers, however, skill at arms must be second nature. How do SAS troopers compare with the soldiers of other elite units when it comes to proficiency with small arms and support weapons?

This chapter will compare the weapon requirements, weapons philosophy, weapons and weapons training of the SAS with those of other elite units, specifically the Australian and New Zealand SAS, the Royal Marines Mountain and Arctic Warfare Cadre, the Green Berets and the SEALs. It will not compare the SAS with those elite units which, when deployed, fight as conventional light infantry, such as the British Paras, the Royal Marines, the US Rangers and the French Foreign Legion. Neither will it cover the weapons of hostage-rescue – these are dealt with in the Counter-Terrorism Chapter.

The Regiment instructs its men in a wide variety of small arms, from the current British Army assault rifle, the SA-80, to Russian and Chinese weapons (David Stirling, the founder of the SAS, insisted that his soldiers should be proficient in the use of enemy weapons so that they could operate behind enemy lines for long periods without re-supply, using captured items). But before the SAS and other elite units accept a weapon into use, they demand that it fulfils a number of requirements. What are they?

A heavily camouflaged SAS sniper takes aim with an L96A1 sniping rifle. In the hands of an expert this weapon is lethal up to a range of 1000m.

Above all, personal weapons must be reliable: one non-functional firearm may jeopardise the safety of a whole SAS team. Personal weapons of elite units must also be capable of putting down concentrated firepower in a relatively short space of time, and to achieve this the assault rifles used by special forces troops have a number of modes of fire – semi-automatic, three-round burst and full-automatic. Finally, any weapon that is carried by elite units must be robust: units may have to operate in hostile terrain – snow, mud, sand and rock – where weapons will be subjected to a lot of wear and tear and temperature extremes. Weapons that work under such conditions are worth their weight in gold. The World War II Sten gun, for example, was widely use by the SAS in the 1940s. It worked well in adverse weather conditions, was easy to strip and maintain and was virtually indestructible if well looked after

Personal weapons must also be compatible with the unit's role. Submachine guns, which are short-range, compact and have a high volume of fire, are fine for hostage-rescue work, but they expend too much ammunition to be used on extended operations, and they are useless for long-range shooting. SAS patrols, for example, carry weapons that are suited to long-range reconnaissance work: light and reliable but packing sufficient firepower to enable the patrol to win the firefight and break contact.

The raiding party was tasked with destroying the aircraft

For those units that operate behind the lines, be they SAS, Green Berets or SEALs, the weapons philosophy is the same: create shock fire support to break enemy resistance and suppress hostile fire to allow the assault elements to close with their targets; and in the defence break up an attack at range – it is the only way small teams can survive contact with larger groups.

The SAS raid on Pebble Island during the 1982 Falklands War provides an excellent example of the weapons philosophy of the Regiment. The airfield on the island, off the north coast of West Falkland, posed a threat to the proposed landing site at San Carlos Bay, East

Falkland. The SAS was sent in to destroy the Argentinian ground-attack aircraft stationed there. The operation, codenamed 'Prelim', called for two groups to provide support for the raiding party, while another would seal off the approaches to the airfield. An additional fire group escorted the raiding party to the airfield and acted as a reserve, ready to react to any Argentinian anti-ambush party that may have been waiting. The raiding party was tasked with destroying the aircraft with explosive charges and M72 LAWs (Light Anti-tank Weapons). Heavier support for the raid was provided by an 81mm mortar and naval gunfire from HMS *Glamorgan* lying offshore.

The initial barrage blew great holes in the farmhouse

Once the 45 men of D Squadron, 22 SAS, were ashore they moved quickly to the airfield and opened up with a devastating barrage of small-arms and anti-tank fire, supported by mortar and naval shells. Very soon the aircraft were wrecked beyond repair and the SAS soldiers were on their way back to the carrier *Hermes*. The only opposition they encountered was some small-arms fire from the Argentinian defenders, though this was soon silenced by a hail of rounds from the SAS troopers. The employment of fast, accurate fire at Pebble Island is typical of the Regiment's use of weapons. How does this compare with the weapons philosophy of other elite units?

The Royal Marines Mountain and Arctic Warfare Cadre has a similar philosophy to that of the Special Air Service. In defence, for example, the emphasis is on a high degree of marksmanship to break up an attack at a range where the enemy's fire is ineffective. In attack, the emphasis is on fast, accurate fire. An excellent example of the Cadre's use of weapons is the assault during the Falklands War on Top Malo House, an isolated farm some 20km northwest of Bluff Cove, East Falkland. The farm was occupied by 16 men of the Argentinian Special Forces, and was in the path of the advancing 3 Para and 42 Commando, both of which were edging their way towards Stanley. In

a daring plan 19 men of the Cadre, led by Captain Rod Boswell, assaulted it on the morning of 31 May 1982. It was at that time beyond British artillery range and no Harrier aircraft could be spared for a ground-attack run.

The Marines were divided into two groups for the attack. One group comprised a seven-man fire section armed with one L42 sniper rifle (a Lee-Enfield .303in rifle fitted with telescopic sights), three Self-Loading Rifles (SLRs), three M16 assault rifles, three M79 grenade launchers and eight LAWs); the other 12 members of the team formed an assault group. The plan was simple: the fire group would pour heavy, concentrated fire into the buildings and then the assault group would skirmish down from its start line to finish off any surviving defenders.

The initial barrage blew great holes in the farmhouse and flushed out the defenders, who

Above: SAS soldiers field-stripping Italian and German weapons in 1942. The SAS insists on its men learning how to use the opposition's weapons.

withdrew into a gully in front of the house. The assault group then began its attack, firing controlled bursts as the Argentinians returned fire. Then the fire group moved forward and peppered the Argentinians with small-arms fire. After losing five dead, the enemy surrendered, signalling the end of a superb action, which was won by a combination of daring and skill at arms.

The US Green Berets operate in larger detachments than their SAS counterparts – 12-man A Teams – which can lay down a formidable amount of firepower in action. However, the weapons philosophy is the same as that of the SAS: shock action to break enemy resistance and suppress enemy fire. If Green Berets are working with insurgent forces, the size of the force will be larger: 24-30-man patrols. In 1966, for example, during the Vietnam War, an American spy plane was lost over Cambodia and the 5th Special Forces Group was ordered to retrieve the aircraft's black box flight recorder. It was retrieved by forming a mobile guerrilla force, comprising a 12-man A Team and 250 Cambodian White Khmer fighters. The force stormed the Viet Cong camp which held the box and accompanied its mission without any loss. During the 1991 Gulf War, Special Forces soldiers operated in smaller units – eight-man patrols – while carrying out road watch missions in western Iraq (surveillance operations usually require smaller-sized teams, which means the chances of being compromised are reduced).

The choice of weapons for special forces operations is very important

The weapons philosophy of the Australian and New Zealand special forces is similar to that of the SAS. It is primarily dictated by the constraints that reconnaissance units face when undertaking long stays behind enemy lines without support from local partisans. In these circumstances, the main considerations are the conservation of ammunition, the adoption of firing stances that afford better control of small arms when firing, accurate shooting in contact situations, and the capturing of foreign weapons to counter ammunition shortfalls.

What of the elite unit weapons themselves? How do those used by the SAS compare to those used by other special forces formations? The choice of weapons for special forces operations is very important, and units have spent a great deal of time and energy in determining which firearms are best suited to their missions. Inevitably, no single weapon can fulfil all the requirements of a unit like the SAS. No weapon can have long range, stopping power, anti-armour capabilities, while being robust, reliable, compact, lightweight and easy to maintain in the field. Therefore, elite units tend to use a variety of weapons, each one tailored to a specific role but, it is hoped, also able to fulfil a variety of tasks if need be.

Above: All elite soldiers spend hours on ranges perfecting their shooting skills. Here, a US Navy SEAL engages targets with a light machine gun.

British and US special forces troops currently favour the M16 assault rifle, fitted with an M203 grenade launcher. The SAS has used the M16 since its campaign in Borneo (1963-66), finding that its attributes are well suited to the Regiment's operations. It is shorter and lighter than the SLR and its low recoil makes it comfortable to fire. During the Pebble Island raid, for example, the raiding party were equipped with M16s, each man carrying three spare magazines plus 200 rounds of spare ammunition.

The latest version of the M16 is the M16A2. The American version is capable of three-round bursts as well as single-shot fire, but in order to prevent the waste of ammunition in battle it does not have a full-automatic facility. The Canadian model can fire full-automatic and single-shot but has no three-round burst facility. The rifle has limited usefulness in desert conditions, because it does not have the range of the SLR and encounters problems in sandy conditions. Nevertheless, it performed well enough in the hands of SAS troopers in Kuwait and Iraq during the Second Gulf War, because SAS men were particularly careful to ensure that their weapons were clean and free of sand (the M16 was originally sold as a self-cleaning weapon).

The M16 has less stopping power than larger-calibre rifles, a fact that was brought home during the assault on Top Malo House by members of the Royal Marines Mountain and Arctic Warfare Cadre during the Falklands War (see above). The commander of the British troops, Captain Rod Boswell, shot an Argentinian soldier four times with his M16 assault rifle. The Argentinian, still alive, then surrendered, causing Boswell to reflect on the lack of real punch of the M16's 5.56mm round when compared with the SLR's 7.62mm bullet.

The M203 grenade launcher is a significant force multiplier when fitted to an M16, and it is this combination that is employed by the SAS. It is not hard to see why: at a stroke it increases a patrol's firepower enormously, and it can fire a variety of high explosive and anti-personnel grenades. It is also useful if a patrol is ambushed, because it can lay down heavy firepower at short notice, enabling the patrol to withdraw. However, it is mainly as a fragmentation weapon for raiding that the M203 is employed by the SAS, hence its use on Pebble Island.

The M16/M203 combination is currently employed by many Western special forces units, though until quite recently the British and Australian SAS preferred the 7.62mm SLR, even for jungle operations, where long-range fire is often impossible. The qualities that endeared the SLR to SAS troopers were its reliability, great robustness and ability to operate in adverse weather conditions.

Below: A British special forces night firing exercise. Accurate night shooting requires a very high level of small arms proficiency.

How does the M16 measure up? It is light and lethal at short ranges, though it has to be kept clean and it cannot withstand rough handling. Nevertheless, in the final analysis its use by a large number of elite units indicates the good outweighs the bad.

Russia's elite Spetsnaz soldiers are armed with the AK-74

Another rifle that is employed by the British SAS, and also by the Australian SAS, is the Steyr AUG. A futuristic design, this 5.56mm bullpup assault rifle is capable of semi- and full-automatic fire and can also be fitted with a three-round burst option (British SLRs were capable of semi-automatic fire only). It is accurate, reliable and can take a lot of punishment – essential qualities for special forces operations. In addition, the weapon can be turned into anything from a submachine gun to a light support weapon by simply swapping parts. Useful attributes include a clear plastic magazine, which allows the firer to see how many rounds he has left. As an assault rifle it is head and shoulders above the M16.

Russia's elite Spetsnaz soldiers are armed with the AK-74 assault rifle or the version with the folding butt, the AKS-74. These weapons are descendants of the famous Kalashnikov AK-47. The AK-74 has an effective muzzle brake that allows accurate burst fire without the muzzle moving away from the line-of-sight, which, combined with the low recoil, makes it an accurate weapon. Like their western counterparts, Russia's special forces have opted for a smaller calibre: 5.45mm compared with the AK-47's 7.62mm. The AK-74 is a better weapon than the M16, if only because it works in all weathers and can take a lot of punishment.

The US Navy's SEALs and the US Army's Special Forces use a similar range of weapons to the SAS, such as M16 assault rifles and M203 grenade launchers, though SEALs have a problem in that their role of underwater insertion makes it difficult to ensure that weapons are still able to work after being immersed in water. A range of weapons produced in competition by Heckler & Koch and Colt can be fired underwater or on land, though details are as yet classified. However, they all appear to be silenced.

The weapon that is most associated with the SAS is the Heckler & Koch MP5 submachine gun, a weapon that is also popular with other elite units, among them the Australian SAS, Delta Force, the SEALs and the SBS. It is used primarily for counter-terrorist duties, and it will be dealt with in more detail in the Counter-Terrorism Chapter.

Sniping is integral to special forces missions, both on the battlefield and in counter-terrorist or hostage-rescue scenarios. The reasons for this are obvious: a sniper or snipers can disrupt enemy troop movements by pinning down units and killing their commanders and communications specialists. As well as killing key enemy personnel, snipers can also inflict material damage on enemy radars and missile sites – one well-aimed shot can turn a missile into a bomb.

The current SAS sniping rifle is the Accuracy International PM

The current SAS sniper rifle is the Accuracy International PM, a 7.62mm calibre rifle that has a plastic stock, a light bipod and a monopod in the butt which allows the rifle to be laid on the target for long periods without the firer having to support the weight of the weapon. The PM, which is designated L96A1, is a bolt-action weapon that fires ammunition fed either from a 10-round magazine, or fed singly through the ejection port when the bolt is pulled back. It is accurate up to a range of 1000m; Accuracy International also make a suppressed version of the rifle that is accurate up to a range of 300m.

US Special Forces and SEALs are equipped with the M24 sniper rifle, a bolt-action 7.62mm weapon that has an adjustable butt and, like the PM, includes composite materials in its furniture. It is every bit as good as the Accuracy International. The Australian and New Zealand SAS favour the Parker Hale 85 sniper rifle, which is probably better than the PM for accuracy and robustness. The Spetsnaz sniper rifle, the Dragunov, is very accurate but rather cumbersome. It is certainly inferior to the PM.

Above: The SLR, a weapon thay has served the SAS well in the humid jungles of the Far East, the deserts of Arabia and the wastes of the Arctic.

Besides rifles, elite forces also need fire-support weapons. The machine gun has played an important part in elite unit operations since World War II. Machine guns provide small-sized patrols with fire support for tactical manoeuvres and destructive firepower for raiding parties. The main disadvantage of the machine gun for elite units that undertake long-range patrol work is the large amount of ammunition it needs – a weapon with a cyclic rate of fire of 750-1000 rounds per minute, for example, expends a lot of ammunition in an engagement. Though the load is usually distributed among individual patrol members, each man can end up carrying a formidable burden. For example, each man could be carrying up to 1000 rounds of machine-gun ammunition, in addition to personal weapons and equipment.

The most favoured machine gun in the SAS inventory is the general purpose machine gun (GPMG), which was first introduced in 1957, and has accompanied the Regiment on all its campaigns ever since. Reliable, robust and accurate, it is fitted with a bipod for the light role and can also be mounted on a tripod for the sustained-fire role. The GPMG was employed effectively at the Battle of Mirbat against PFLOAG guerrillas (see below). How does it compare with other machine guns?

The machine guns of other elite units include the US M60 and the German Heckler & Koch 21 (both used by the Green Berets and

Above: The British bullpup SA-80. It is lighter and more compact than the SLR, but its 5.56mm round lacks the stopping power of a 7.62mm bullet.

SEALs), the German MG3 (German Mountain Troops) and the Minimi (US Marine Corps). The M60 suffers from the same problems as all GPMGs: too light for the squad role but not heavy enough for platoon/company-level tasks. It has also suffered from reliability and operating problems. The MG3, a modern version of the

World War II MG42, is reliable, accurate and has a high rate of fire (1200rpm). It is a better weapon than the GPMG. The Heckler & Koch 21 is accurate and can be fired easily from the hip. However it lacks the range of the GPMG.

The problem of weight versus firepower has been addressed by several manufacturers in the last few years, with the result that there is now a range of machine guns available that are lighter than their predecessors. This has obvious advantages for small special forces foot patrols.

During the 1991 Gulf War the SAS Road Watch patrols were equipped with Minimi machine guns, one of the new so-called 'mini-GPMGs' that are currently available. The weapon weighs 6.8kg, four kilos less than the GPMG. An unusual feature of the Minimi is that it can use either a box magazine or belt feed without modification. The gun has a heavy, quick-change barrel and a neat folding bipod. It has proved a popular weapon, being very reliable and easy to fire. Though its 5.56mm ammunition may lack the punch of the 7.62mm round, the Regiment likes the saving in weight, and it is particularly appreciated by those who have to travel long distances on foot. More importantly, it is very reliable, just like the GPMG.

Elite units also employ heavier support weapons, which can add substantially to the firepower of an attack, or reinforce defence if necessary. But long-range patrols on foot cannot carry heavy weapons such as large mortars and field pieces. Nevertheless, advances in technology have resulted in some systems – such as light anti-tank weapons – that weigh less than 5kg, making them much more suitable for elite unit operations.

Anti-tank weapons in SAS and US elite forces use include the M72, a reliable weapon that was used to devastating effect during the Pebble Island raid. A throw-away system, it weighs only 2.36kg and can penetrate armour up to 700mm thick. Milan, a larger anti-armour weapon, has a range of 2000m and can penetrate armour up to 1060mm thick. Its one drawback is its weight: the whole system weighs over 16kg, with the missiles weighing 6.65kg each. This means that it is almost impossible for SAS teams on deep-penetration missions to carry Milans

with them. Milans were used by the SAS in the Falklands, when D Squadron made a diversionary attack on Argentinian positions on 20 May 1982 to cover the main British landings at San Carlos Water. One of the troopers who took part in the action remembers the problems: 'We stopped regularly to adjust our bergens, as well as the Milans we were carrying. The weight was unbelievable. I remember thinking it was a good job we were going to fire most of the ammo because I for one didn't fancy the idea of marching back with it.' A similar system is the

Below: Put an M203 grenade launcher on an assault rifle and what do you get? A significant force multiplier. These SEALs appreciate the point.

Spetsnaz AT-4 'Spigot' anti-tank weapon, though it can only penetrate 600mm of armour.

Modern man-portable surface-to-air missiles (SAMs) mean that elite teams, especially vehicle columns, can protect themselves from air attack. One such system in SAS and US use is the American Stinger SAM, which was used by the Regiment to shoot down an Argentinian Pucara aircraft on 21 May 1982 during the Falklands War. Equipped with an infra-red guidance system, Stinger has a range of 5km.

The High Power's compactness makes it suitable for plain-clothes work

Handguns are primarily used by elite units for counter-terrorist duties and hostage-rescue operations. However, they are also carried by soldiers on extended operations, in addition to their assault rifles and machine guns. Though the qualities that elite units look for in handguns are many and varied, the prime considerations are always accuracy and first-time reliability. The most popular handgun in the British, Australian and New Zealand SAS is the Browning High Power, a semi-automatic model that has a magazine capacity of 14 rounds.

The current version of the High Power in SAS service, the Mark 3, meets all the Regiment's handgun requirements: it is reliable and safe, and it has a high-capacity magazine. Its compactness is particularly suitable for plain-clothes work in Northern Ireland, and it can be operated with either the left or right hand. It has a rapid magazine-change function, speedy operation and aiming, and works well in adverse weather conditions.

Other popular elite unit handguns include the M1911 (SEALs and Green Berets), the Smith and Wesson .357 Magnum (Delta Force) and the Beretta 92 (US Marine Corps). The M1911 is very similar to the High Power, being robust and reliable. The Magnum is a hand-held cannon, but being a revolver has only a six-round magazine – a major drawback in a firefight. The Beretta is a superb combat handgun, though there have been technical problems that have resulted in the SEALs abandoning it and going back to the M1911.

Weapons form one half of the equation when it comes to elite unit firepower, the other half is made up by the handling skills of the troops using them. Because elite teams operate alone and often behind enemy lines, their employment of small arms differs from the tactical use of weapons in conventional units. The troops of the former Soviet Union, for example, were taught not to shoot at individual targets with their AK-47 assault rifles. They were instructed to employ them as part of a mass barrage of fire that would overwhelm the enemy. The emphasis in elite units, on the other hand, is on fast, accurate fire that quickly establishes an advantage and either allows the patrol to withdraw safely or breaks up a hostile assault well before enemy fire becomes effective.

Studies have shown that in battle many soldiers fail to fire their weapons

How does SAS weapons training compare with the training in other elite units? The first step is to train the men so that they actually fire their weapons in combat. This may seem slightly ludicrous, but studies have shown that in battle many soldiers do fail to do so. In Korea, for example, when United Nations patrols were ambushed by the Chinese, it is estimated that less than 10 per cent of those ambushed fired their weapons. Studies have also shown that only 15 per cent of infantrymen fired their weapons in any particular engagement. In addition, of those men who do open fire in combat, most, because of fear, stress and fatigue, discharge their weapons at ranges of under 100m, and most of the shots they fire are inaccurate. In the light of these statistics, the need for special training in this area becomes readily apparent.

SAS standard operating procedures (SOPs) concerning firing weapons stress the importance of identifying a target before opening fire and the necessity of moving into tactical situations quickly, a philosophy that is echoed in almost all other elite units. The head-on contact drill, for example, was devised for a four-man patrol while on the move. When contact is made with the enemy, each team member moves reactively into a position that allows him to fire at the opposition without hitting a comrade. Thus, if the patrol is moving in file, the three men behind the lead scout will break left and right and bring their weapons to bear on the enemy.

It is the same for the Australians. As a result of Allied commando experiences in World War II and general SAS experience in Malaya, Australian SAS instructors now teach recruits body-line shooting, whereby the firer points the weapon without aiming and discharges two shots (a double tap) into the upper body of an enemy soldier. This method conserves ammunition, is faster than taking careful aim, and allows better control of a recoiling weapon. It can be used regardless of whether a trooper is carrying an assault rifle, handgun, submachine gun, shotgun or machine gun.

The first few seconds of an armed contact are critical

Such drills require intensive training in the handling and firing of different types of firearms, until handling a weapon becomes second nature. To this end, SAS soldiers spend a great deal of time on ranges, where they reach a degree of proficiency in the handling of a variety of weapons that is far above that found in conventional units. In addition, there is the hostage-rescue drill practised in the 'Killing House' at Hereford, where students are put through a number of scenarios which test to the limit their skills in the handling of handguns, submachine guns and shotguns. All this training has one aim: to produce a soldier who can correctly identify and hit a target in a split second. In addition, troopers receive intensive instruction in the maintenance and stripping of weapons, so that every weapon will work first time every time.

Other drills taught to elite soldiers include keeping weapons to hand at all times (the first few seconds of a contact are critical, and not having the means to instigate rapid return fire is fatal), keeping them clean at all times, and learning how to deal with jams and stoppages. Other 'tricks of the trade' include having tracer rounds as the last two bullets in a magazine. When the first tracer is fired the second round is automatically chambered, thus the firer knows

instantly when to change magazines and that he has another round in the breech.

The results of such training can be dramatic. For example, an SAS trooper can draw, aim and fire a full magazine from a High Power in under three seconds. A similar degree of proficiency is achieved with assault rifles, submachine guns and machine guns – a result of the hundreds of hours spent on ranges and stripping and reassembling a host of weapons.

The Royal Marines Mountain and Arctic Warfare Cadre includes marksmanship and weapons handling in the initial selection process on the ML2 Course (see Selection and Training Chapter), and each man is expected to display high proficiency with all the Cadre's weapons.

The Cadre's one major shortcoming is the lack of training with foreign weapons. This would have resulted in serious problems if its men had ever been involved in a NATO-Warsaw Pact conflict. Trained to conduct long-range reconnaissance missions, individuals would soon have found themselves deep behind enemy lines. It was envisaged they would have been guided to friendly territory by partisans and other special forces troops. Nevertheless, if a Cadre member had lost his weapon or run out of ammunition, only unfamiliar enemy examples would have been available.

The attack was quickly broken up by accurate shooting

The Green Berets devote a lot of time to weapons training. Its weapons specialist course involves the use of a wide range of small arms and support weapons (handguns, rifles, submachine guns, grenade launchers, mortars, rocket launchers and anti-tank and anti-aircraft missile launchers). There is also instruction in the use of over 60 foreign weapons. As they will be instructors, all operatives must be proficient in marksmanship, weapons maintenance and repair, as well as the tactical use of weapons in raids and ambushes. The Americans are also very adept at incorporating battlefield support systems, such as artillery and air strikes.

A classic episode showing Green Beret expertise with small arms took place during the fire and 40mm grenades launched from M203s. Though an F-16 aircraft then aided the Green Berets by launching a series of ground attacks against subsequent Iraqi assaults, the marksmanship of the Americans was a crucial part of the battle, because it broke up the Iraqi attack.

The US counter-terrorist unit Delta Force members spend many hours on weapons training. Four hours daily, four days a week are devoted to weapons skills, though because of their hostage-rescue duties individuals divide this time equally between range work and the 'House of Horrors' (similar to the SAS's 'Killing House'). Delta Team members display a high degree of marksmanship with their firearms at what is generally considered to be the extreme ranges of their weapons.

The defences consisted of flat-topped houses and mud-walled forts

The weapons proficiency of the Australian SAS is also very high. In a firefight its men will shoot quickly and accurately, even if they are ambushed. This skill at arms was to result in some spectacular successes during the Vietnam War. In five years, the Australian and New Zealand SAS killed over 500 Viet Cong for the loss of only one man killed and 27 wounded.

What of the SEALs? Due to their counter-terrorist brief, and the training conducted to support that role, they must be considered more highly trained in this field than the Green Berets and on a par with the various SAS.

There is one more aspect to elite unit weapons training: night firing. Because most raids and ambushes are conducted under cover of darkness, night shooting is a central feature of special forces weapons training. At night most soldiers have a tendency to fire over the top of a poorly lit target in a firefight. Regular night shooting practice corrects this, and it also ensures that night ambushes do not result in fatalities caused by friendly fire.

The motto of 22 SAS Training Wing is 'Train Hard, Fight Easy'. This philosophy has resulted in training that is punishing, but which ensures that individuals will function properly in combat, and fire their weapons accurately. This

Above: One of the assault rifles used by the Australian SAS – the Steyr AUG. Its fragile looks belie a weapon that is almost indestructible.

1991 Gulf War, when an eight-man Special Forces team was inserted into southern Iraq to conduct surveillance on Highway Eight. Unfortunately, the area was a hive of civilian activity, and the Americans were soon discovered. The team set up a defensive position along a canal near the highway. Up to 200 Iraqi soldiers, supported by paramilitaries, arrived and launched an attack across the open ground between the canal and the highway. However, it was quickly broken up by accurate small-arms

Above: Two SAS soldiers on the range with a tried and trusted friend: the GPMG. Robust and reliable, it has been in SAS service for nearly 40 years.

gives them the edge when it comes to confronting conventional troops or irregular units in battle, and has resulted in spectacular victories. The SAS defence of the Omani town of Mirbat in July 1972 is perhaps the best example of the Regiment's weapons skills in action, and it is worth recording in detail. There are many similarities between this action and the defence of the camp at Nam Dong by a US Special Forces team during the Vietnam War.

Mirbat is a small coastal town in western Oman, located 56km east of the provincial

capital, Salalah. In July 1972 it was defended by a nine-man SAS team, commanded by 23-year-old Captain Mike Kealy, 30 *askars* (tribesmen) and 25 gendarmes. Kealy was untried in battle, and was known by his men as a 'baby Rupert' ('Rupert' is SAS slang for officer), but he would prove himself to be a fine leader of men. There were also some *firqat* (Dhofari irregulars trained

armed with aged bolt-action Lee-Enfield rifles, while the SAS were equipped with a variety of small arms – SLRs, M16s and L42 sniper rifles. The defenders' heavier weapons included a 25-pounder field gun in a sandbagged pit beside the Gendarmerie Fort, an 81mm mortar in a sandbagged pit beside the Batthouse, and a GPMG and 0.5in Browning heavy machine gun on the roof of the Batthouse itself.

Donlon inherited a potentially explosive situation

The enemy, the so-called *adoo*, were guerrillas of the People's Front for the Liberation of the Occupied Arabian Gulf (PFLOAG), an organisation that was attempting to establish a communist regime in Oman. The force they had outside Mirbat possessed considerably more firepower and numbers than the defenders: 250 guerrillas armed with Soviet assault rifles and supported by 75mm recoilless rifles, rocket launchers and mortars In addition, the attack had been timed to coincide with the monsoon period, which meant low cloud and rain. This would make it difficult for the Omani Air Force to mount ground-attack missions in support of Mirbat. There was one thing in the SAS's favour, though: the terrain was open and relatively flat, which meant uninterrupted fields of fire for the guns of the defenders.

For both sides the assault on Mirbat was a watershed. For the *adoo*, it was a golden opportunity to discredit the Omani government's civil aid programme. This was beginning to take effect in Dhofar – by the end of 1971 the government had made substantial gains: 700 Dhofaris fighting in *firqats* and the coastal plain and towns under government control. However, if the rebels could achieve a victory, they would persuade those wavering Dhofaris that the government's cause was lost (in a warrior society military prowess is very highly rated). Similarly, once the SAS realised that the assault being mounted against Mirbat represented a major *adoo* effort, there was a great incentive to defeat it and damage the *adoo*'s cause, perhaps mortally.

The Green Berets' defence of the camp at Nam Dong in the central northern Thua Thien

by the SAS) in the town, but 60 of them had been despatched to the mountain escarpment that overlooked the town to investigate an enemy sighting: their absence had weakened the garrison substantially.

The defences consisted of flat-topped houses and mud-walled forts: the Wali's Fort (occupied by the *askars*), the Dhofar Gendarmerie Fort (containing the gendarmes) and the Batthouse (SAS HQ). The town and the forts were protected by a barbed wire cattle fence around the perimeter. The gendarmes and *askars* were

Province in the north of the Republic of Vietnam had taken place eight years earlier. The camp blocked Viet Cong (VC) infiltration routes into the lowlands around Da Nang and Phu Bai. It was one of the camps established under the so-called Civilian Irregular Defense Group (CIDG) Program, which was a joint US/Vietnamese Special Forces effort to enlist the support of the Montagnards, the inhabitants of the Vietnamese Central Highlands, and thus deny the region to the Viet Cong. Because of its location Nam Dong was considered too isolated, and so US Special Forces Detachment A-726 (11 Americans and one Australian), plus its commander,

Below: The Stinger hand-held surface-to-air missile, as used by the SAS (in the Falklands one shot down a Pucara aircraft) and American elite units.

Captain Roger Donlon, was detailed to close it down in July 1964.

The situation around and inside the camp, however, left a lot to be desired, and Donlon inherited a potentially explosive scenario. The villagers in the valley were hostile to the American advisors and the remote location meant reinforcements could not be called up quickly. To compound all these problems, the camp itself had been neglected, and high, thick elephant grass had been allowed to grow up to the very edge of the barbed wire of the outer perimeter. This provided cover for enemy soldiers to infiltrate themselves up to the perimeter fence prior to their assault.

The camp itself was a former French outpost and consisted of an inner and outer perimeter and a small airstrip located just

beyond the barbed wire. Donlon's A Team occupied the inner perimeter, together with 50 Nungs (mercenaries of Chinese extraction), who were loyal to the Western advisors. The outer perimeter was occupied by 381 South Vietnamese CIDG personnel, with 5000 Montagnards living beyond the wire.

Tension between the CIDG irregulars and Nungs reached crisis point on 5 July, culminating in a rock-throwing incident over a camp prostitute. That night the Nungs remained at their posts, fearful of what the irregulars would do.

In the early hours of 6 July, a reinforced Viet Cong battalion – some 1000 men – crossed the airstrip and silenced a 21-man outpost near the airfield. The VC then used the elephant grass as cover to reach the outer perimeter. The VC were armed with AK-47 assault rifles and were backed up by mortars, while the Americans and their 'allies' were armed with AR-15 assault rifles (an early version of the M16), together with M60 machine guns. Two factors were in Donlon's favour: the Nungs were at their posts before the battle began and the camp was well-stocked with

Above: Milan, an anti-tank weapon that was used to devastating effect by the SAS in the Falklands, when D Squadron 'brassed up' Goose Green.

ammunition. However, when the enemy attack was launched it was a total surprise.

This was not the case at Mirbat. The focal point of the *adoo* attack was the DG Fort. As it dominated the town and the small airstrip, it was the key to the battle. However, the enemy's stealthy approach was compromised when a firefight developed between the guerrillas and a small force of gendarmes at 0530 hours on 19 July 1972, which resulted in the defenders manning their posts. Very soon mortar shells and machine-gun fire were being directed at the DG Fort, the Batthouse and the Wali's Fort, while enemy infantry groups were also advancing towards the DG Fort.

Kealy gave the order for the SAS mortar to open fire, and then he and the other SAS soldiers opened up with a mixture of machine guns and assault rifles. The SLRs, GPMGs and Brownings found their marks with aimed shots

Above: Captain Roger Donlon surveys the scene at Nam Dong after the Viet Cong attack. His conduct in the battle won him the Medal of Honor.

and bursts. SAS training was paying dividends as the ground became littered with dead *adoo*. In addition, SAS men were firing the 25-pounder in the gun-pit beside the DG Fort. The efforts of Corporal Labalaba manning the field gun were the stuff of legend: he continued to fire the gun despite being badly wounded, loading shell after shell into the breech, until he was hit a second time and died instantly; he was Mentioned in Despatches for his efforts. The gendarmes and *askars* were also firing, though being less well trained and armed, their fire was less effective.

As the battle continued, the intensity of *adoo* fire increased, a lethal cocktail of machine-gun fire, rockets and mortar rounds was directed at Mirbat itself, the Batthouse, the DG Fort and the Wali's Fort. Kealy was surrounded on three

sides, and his requests for air support and reinforcements to be sent from Salalah became frantic. Two of the SAS men were killed and two more were wounded. The fire from the mortar pit and Batthouse continued, but the *adoo* were gaining ground.

The appearance of two Omani Strikemaster jets stemmed the *adoo*, plus reinforcements in the shape of 24 members of G Squadron, 22 SAS, turned the tide and the attack was defeated. However, it was the fire from the Batthouse, supplemented by the mortar and 25-pounder, that had been the key to victory.

At Nam Dong, however, Donlon had no opportunity to try and break up the enemy attack at long range, because the VC were already at the outer perimeter wire by the time their mortars opened up at 0230 hours on 6 July 1964. At a stroke the mortar rounds destroyed the Nung barracks, camp dispensary and communications shack, though not before the signaller had sent a message stating they were under intense mortar attack and calling for reinforcements. Then the command bunker was hit and started to burn. For Donlon the end appeared to be imminent.

When the mortars stopped the first wave of VC cut the wire fence, stormed forward and engaged in hand-to-hand combat with the CIDG irregulars. The Australian advisor, Warrant Officer Kevin Conway was shot dead, and the VC fought their way to the inner perimeter.

The crisis point of the battle had been reached, but the situation was saved by the weapons skills of the Green Berets. There were two 81mm mortar positions near the main gate, one manned by Staff Sergeant Michael Disser, the other by Staff Sergeant Merwin Woods. Woods in particular proved expert at 'walking' a line of mortar fire around the perimeter, blowing VC detachments to pieces. In addition, Sergeant John Houston was manning an M60 machine gun from a mound of earth, using controlled, accurate bursts to stem the enemy's advance, until he was killed by VC fire. The enemy then attempted to blow the main gate.

The battle had lasted five hours, but the camp had not fallen

Donlon and another Green Beret shot dead the sappers attempting to lay the charges, but they themselves were then forced to retire. An hour had now elapsed since the VC attack started, but there was no let-up in the fighting. By this time two of Donlon's men had been killed, in addition to many CIDG and Nungs, and Donlon himself had been wounded. Yet still the Green Berets continued to direct the battle, inflicting casualties on the enemy with controlled AR-15 fire from defensive positions.

Donlon was in one of the mortar pits with three of his men, and the group became the target of intensive VC attacks. Grenades rained down on them and they were forced to pick them up and throw them back. Donlon then gave the order to retire and the team fell back, though not before another Green Beret had been killed. Donlon, wounded four times, continued to direct the camp's defence until reinforcements, in the shape of six Marine helicopters carrying Special Forces troops, landed at 0745 hours. The battle had lasted five hours, but the camp had not fallen. A heavy price had been paid: one Australian and two Americans dead, seven Americans wounded, 50 CIDG and Nungs killed. There were 150 dead VC in and around the perimeter at Nam Dong.

Of the two actions, the SAS defence of Mirbat was the more crucial

At both Mirbat and Nam Dong individual special forces soldiers maintained accurate fire throughout the battle. In addition, each man kept his rifle or machine gun working. In battle barrels get hot, weapons jam and working parts get wet and dirty. This can result in stoppages, and slick immediate action drills are required to rectify the problem. When there are only a handful of men, one non-working weapon reduces overall firepower significantly, perhaps fatally. At Nam Dong the Green Berets were the decisive factor in the battle, even though they constituted less than one per cent of the total number of combatants; likewise the SAS team at Mirbat, where they constituted three per cent of the total number of combatants engaged.

Of the two actions, the SAS defence of Mirbat was the more crucial. The camp at Nam Dong was being closed down anyway, and although a VC victory would have resulted in a dent in American prestige, this would have been temporary, and certainly would not have resulted in the collapse of the US war effort throughout South Vietnam. On the other hand, had Mirbat fallen the morale and standing of the *adoo* would have soared. As it was, the SAS victory marked a major turning point in the insurgency war. No other elite unit can make such a claim regarding its weapons skills. At Mirbat the SAS really did prove they were the world's best.

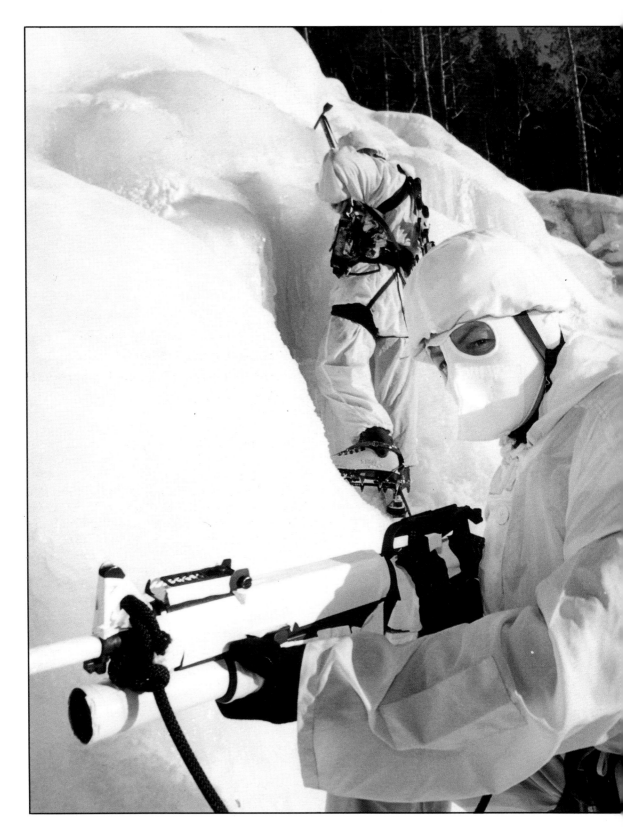

HOSTILE ENVIRON-MENTS

It is a proud boast of the SAS that its men can be deployed to any region of the world at a moment's notice, a claim echoed by other special forces units. But who is the best when it comes to fighting in hostile terrain?

This chapter will examine how SAS soldiers are trained and equipped to fight in the jungle, desert, mountains and Arctic, and will compare these methods with the training and equipment given to other elite soldiers that operate in hostile environments: the men of the Australian and New Zealand SAS, the Royal Marines, the US Marine Corps, the Green Berets, the Canadian Special Service Force and Spetsnaz.

A cursory glance at the SAS Regiment's roll of honour will show that since the Regiment's creation its soldiers have fought in many different types of hostile terrain: deserts (North Africa 1941-43, Oman 1970-76 and Iraq and Kuwait 1990-91); jungle (Malaya 1948-60 and Borneo 1963-66); mountains (Oman 1958-59 and Aden 1964-67); and snow and ice terrain (the Falklands and South Georgia 1982). Today's SAS soldiers are expected to be able to fight in any terrain anywhere in the world, and to be ready to be deployed at a moment's notice. The organisation of the Regiment reflects this requirement. For example, each Sabre Squadron is divided into troops that have a particular speciality: Boat

Well-wrapped members of Britain's Mountain and Arctic Warfare Cadre on an ice climb in Norway. The Cadre often trains SAS soldiers in arctic warfare techniques.

Troop (all aspects of amphibious warfare), Mobility Troop (Land Rovers, fast attack vehicles and motorcycles), Air Troop (freefall parachuting) and Mountain Troop (mountaineering and winter warfare operations). Desert warfare operations are the preserve of the Mobility Troops, and so these soldiers are frequently deployed to the Middle East for training.

How do other elite units compare to the SAS with regard to preparing their men for operations in hostile terrain? Direct comparison is, in many cases, impossible because other

formations do not train to fight in the number of environments that the SAS prepares its men for. The Australian SAS, for example, trains for operations on the Australian mainland and the outlying islands. This means preparing men for missions in desert, sub-tropical shrub, wetland and jungle – they train in Thailand, New Guinea and in the rain forests of Queensland. Arctic terrain training is not high on the agenda.

The British SAS, on the other hand, devotes a great deal of time to training its men for operations in all hostile environments. This

Above: Say cheese! A group of SAS recruits pose for the camera after completing their jungle training in Brunei.

begins during Continuation Training (see Selection and Training Chapter), when the students are given tuition in all aspects of living under such conditions. However, this is very much survival training – building shelters, finding food and water, laying traps and lighting fires – rather than learning how to mount military operations in particular types of hostile

terrain. Nevertheless, it does give the students a basic knowledge on which they can build during their careers with the Special Air Service.

The one environment that SAS soldiers are quickly taught to master is the jungle. Following Continuation Training, prospective SAS recruits undergo jungle training in the Far East (usually Brunei), and it is here that individuals are first introduced to the Regiment's operational tactics in a hostile environment. The course lasts for six weeks, and the candidates are taught basic standard operating procedures (SOPs) and patrol skills. To pass this extremely demanding course students must prove that they have mastered jungle drills, that they are adept at handling and firing weapons at short ranges and in areas of poor visibility, and that they are suited to small-group and long-duration patrols.

'Shoot and scoot' is designed to prevent casualties during an encounter

What type of jungle training do the men receive? Because of poor visibility, engagements in the jungle tend to be at close range. Defeating the opposition in such a situation depends on the ability to move silently, to detect the enemy first and to shoot accurately and quickly at moving targets. Getting into firing positions quickly and making the first shot count are all-important. Individuals are instructed to use the 'Belfast cradle' when on patrol, whereby a man holds his weapon crooked in his forearm when moving, as opposed to slinging it over his shoulder. This pose allows a quicker response to any surprise contacts with the enemy.

Other jungle SOPs include 'shoot and scoot', devised by Lieutenant-Colonel John Woodhouse during the campaign in Malaya. It is designed to prevent casualties during a chance encounter with the enemy. When the contact is made the patrol lays down a heavy barrage of fire, after which the men 'scoot' to a pre-arranged emergency rendezvous.

How skilled is the SAS in jungle warfare? Here is the statement of Major-General Walter Walker, Director of Operations in Borneo during the SAS campaign there: 'I regard 70 troopers of the SAS as being as valuable to me as

700 infantry in the role of "hearts and minds", border surveillance, early warning, stay behind, and eyes and ears with a sting.'

What about other units? The Green Berets undergo less training in hostile terrain than the SAS: although they fought in Vietnam, they undergo jungle training only in cases where the jungle is a central feature of the area of responsibility of the Special Forces Group (SFG) with which they are serving. These areas of responsibility are as follows: 10th SFG concentrates on operations in Europe and Africa, 5th SFG on Southeast Asia and the Pacific, 1st SFG on Northeast Asia, 3rd SFG on Sub-Saharan Africa, 7th SFG on the Caribbean, Central and South America. 11th SFG is the US Army Reserve and based at Fort Meade, Maryland, while 12th SFG (also US Army Reserve) is based at Arlington Heights, Illinois. The remaining two SFGs form part of the Army National Guard – 19th SFG operates out of Salt Lake City, Utah, and the 20th SFG is based in Birmingham, Alabama.

Although the 7th and 5th SFGs may routinely train in jungle, the Green Berets themselves do not actually fight in the jungle. They will be training indigenous troops at a village or barracks. Even in Vietnam, individual CIDG camps (see Weapons Skills Chapter) were well-equipped with many luxury items. In fact, the nearest Green Berets come to SAS jungle training are the annual exercises held in Thailand.

Patrols went out mainly in the daytime, preferring not to work blind

Like its British counterpart, the Australian SAS has an excellent record in jungle warfare. During its campaigns in Borneo and Vietnam in the 1960s and 1970s, it mounted more than 1400 patrols, had 298 contacts with the enemy and killed more than 500, all for the loss of one man who died as a result of wounds sustained in action. This superb record is testimony to the high level of expertise the unit has in jungle warfare techniques. In Vietnam, for example, patrols went out mainly in the daytime, preferring not to work blind. After breakfast there would be a reconnaissance of the immediate area, then the patrol would move stealthily until mid-morning,

when the men would deploy on either side of a track known to be used by the enemy. The SAS men were masters of concealment, and would lie within metres of enemy troops without being noticed. Using a combination of stealth, silence and infinite patience, the SAS troopers would gather valuable information and then vanish into the undergrowth. Tactics included individuals carrying lengths of nylon fishing line, which would be attached to a finger of each patrol member to allow signals to be passed down the line in absolute silence by a gentle tug on the connecting nylon.

Those who pass are awarded Mountain Guide certificates and badges

What about mountain and arctic warfare skills? SAS soldiers attend courses run by the Royal Marines, and they are also sent abroad to learn mountain and arctic techniques. For example, members of 22 SAS (plus the Territorial Army units, 21 and 23 SAS) frequently attend the German Army Mountain and Winter Warfare School at Luttensee, near Mittenwald, Bavaria. The aim of the Army Mountain Guide course that they undertake there is to produce men who can advise commanders on all aspects of mountain warfare and instruct other members of their unit in mountain and arctic skills.

The course begins with an initial selection week, followed by five weeks of intensive rock training at Oberreintal on the Wendelstein. The troops live in tents high in the Bavarian Alps, where they spend up to 10 hours a day conducting climbs. The course then progresses to Chamonix in the French Alps, where the students receive instruction in ice-climbing techniques. During this phase they have to carry out a difficult climbing exercise in the Mont Blanc area to stay on the course.

Skiing is also taught on the course, and this can prove to be difficult for the SAS soldiers, many of whom have never skied before in their lives. Nevertheless, after six weeks of ski instruction each candidate must take the German Ski Association's Instructor's Test, after which, if they pass, they spend a further three to four weeks on a high alpine course in the Gran

Paradiso region of Italy. Then it's back to Luttensee for the final test. The passees are awarded Mountain Guide certificates and badges.

How does this compare with the mountain and arctic warfare training given to other units? Britain's Royal Marines have fought in the jungles of the Far East and the mountains of Aden, but their current hostile terrain training emphasises mountain and arctic warfare, since in a NATO-Warsaw Pact war they would have been committed to NATO's northern flank in Norway. Even with the demise of the Warsaw Pact, the Commando Brigade still conducts exercises in Norway, and all personnel taking part must pass the Arctic Warfare Training Course. The three-week course teaches survival and fighting in arctic conditions, and includes elementary skiing tuition given by the Mountain Leaders (MLs) and Military Ski Instructors (MSIs). The MSIs also teach cold-weather survival and the art of building 10- and four-man shelters and snow holes, and the students spend 11 days and four nights in the field.

Above: The Mountain and Winter Warfare School at Luttensee, Bavaria, Germany, where many regular and TA SAS troopers are taught.

Ski-qualified personnel who have not deployed to Norway within the previous 12 months, and those who require any form of refresher training, are required to do a week's Arctic Survival Training. Both these courses are usually run back-to-back during the first month of the Brigade's three-month deployment to Norway.

The three-month training schedule takes place at Mo-i-Rana in Norway, and includes section and individual battle drills, patrolling, camouflage and concealment, ambush and anti-ambush drills, and an exercise in which the commandos play both defenders and aggressors. During this exercise the Special Boat Service (SBS) and Mountain and Arctic Warfare Cadre personnel are infiltrated by land or submarine to perform reconnaissance, raid 'enemy' command posts, cut lines of communication, trap retreating 'enemy' forces, and strike against supply and munitions depots and units of rotary- and fixed-wing aircraft. Special attention was paid to airfields because it was those that the Warsaw Pact would have attacked first because they needed them to dominate the North Atlantic.

The US Marine Corps has a cold weather operational requirement because of the possibility of future conflict in Korea (South Korea is extremely mountainous), the need to be able to undertake 'Out of Area' operations, and the USMC's new special operations/intervention

role. The Corps' Mountain Warfare Training Center is at Pickle Meadows in the Sierra Nevada mountains. It is an all-year facility that conducts cold weather training and skiing in winter and mountaineering and high alpine operations in summer. The centre trains up to 10,000 troops a year, and has 65 instructors: 47 unit operations teachers, 10 mountain leaders,

Below: Two German mountain troops negotiate a snow-covered mountain trail. Note how well their camouflage suits blend into the background.

Above: In arctic terrain, it is imperative that hands and feet are protected from the cold, particularly when handling metal gun barrels and parts.

four cold weather instructors and four survival instructors.

The courses last 28 days and consist of ski instruction, forced marches in the mountains (10km with light packs weighing 13-18kg, and 15km with 22-32kg packs), cold weather and mountain survival, snow and mountain mobility, and how to mount military operations in these environments. On the mountains the training is very realistic, and a lot of Marines are evacuated with frostnip and acute mountain sickness.

For the soldiers of the Canadian Special Service Force (SSF), hostile terrain training focuses on the landscape of northern and western Canada: forest, wetlands and tundra. The annual training cycle includes small arms and support weapons refresher training at one of the three infantry Battle Schools, individual specialisation

refresher training within the unit, and Command Post Exercises and Field Training Exercises, which are usually held in sub-arctic wilderness. These involve the commandos seizing an area for the SSF Battle Group. The commandos' readiness for rapid deployment is assessed on two annual 'rendezvous' exercises, which involve seizing, clearing and holding selected landing zones. Dedicated airborne engineer units then construct the necessary airfields, landing pads, roads and bridges.

The Spetsnaz mission called for an attack on two railway bridges

US Ranger hostile environments training prepares individual Rangers for operations in any terrain in any part of the world. All battalions are rotated through the training cycle, which includes 12 months' mountain training and 18 months' cold weather/arctic training.

Dedicated mountain troops in Germany, Italy and France naturally devote all their training to warfare in rock and snow terrain. For example, some 45 per cent of German Mountain Troops' annual training is carried out actually in the mountains. Such specialisation can produce excellent mountain warriors. Italy's alpine formations contain parachute reconnaissance companies that specialise in parachute drops onto mountains. Meanwhile, the geography of the two islands of New Zealand – there are a plethora of mountains and glaciers – means that New Zealand SAS troopers devote a considerable time to training in ice and mountain environments, and as a result there are many experienced climbers in the squadron.

Russian Spetsnaz soldiers are trained to fight in similar environments to the Canadians: forest, steppe and bog with arctic variations. An account of a Spetsnaz training exercise provided by a defector gives an interesting insight into how the training prepares individuals for operations in hostile regions, and gives some idea of the physical stamina needed by members of this particular elite corps. The mission called for a simulated attack on two railway bridges and some communications centres. As the ground was covered in snow, each man was equipped with white coveralls and skis. A parachute jump was conducted at 2200 hours in the dark. The team assembled, hit the communications centre and then covered 70km by the next afternoon. Using a 'captured' vehicle to journey to the second target, the patrol then hit that target and made its way back to friendly lines. During the course of the exercise the patrol had travelled some 700km on skis. Each man carried only two days' worth of dried food.

The SAS tops the list when it comes to specialist desert training

The desert also figures large in the SAS's hostile environment training. The Regiment's first campaign, conducted by David Stirling in World War II, was waged in the vastness of North Africa, and the SAS has trained its men in desert tactics ever since. Inevitably, because of the distances involved and the need for mobility, this has meant men having to learn desert driving techniques. Prior to the Gulf War, in 1990, D and G Squadrons had held exercises in the Empty Quarter of Saudi Arabia. Vehicles and men were put through punishing routines which were made even tougher by the type of terrain they were conducted in.

The Empty Quarter, or Rub' Al-Khali, is the largest sand desert in the world, unbearably hot in the summer and cold in the dead of winter. The weather and terrain demand that vehicles are driven expertly. For example, when traversing a dune drivers should climb it on foot first to satisfy themselves that their vehicle will not get stuck at the top, that the slopes are not too steep and the sand is not too soft. Tyre pressure can be reduced to give increased traction, though too much driving on partially deflated tyres will result in them overheating. In addition, driving over rocky desert terrain will wear out wheels, springs and shock absorbers. All these problems have to be taken into account when operating with vehicles in the desert.

SAS vehicle training in Saudi Arabia, Oman and the United Arab Emirates keeps the men up to scratch. This paid dividends in the Gulf War against Iraq, when SAS columns roamed behind Iraqi lines and inflicted damage on the enemy.

As well as posing dangers to vehicles, desert driving is also physically exhausting, and the desert itself can be life-threatening. The popular image of a desert is high temperatures, blue sky, no shade and little water. In such conditions soldiers need to guard against dehydration, sunstroke and sunburn, which means covering up and avoiding unnecessary fluid loss. But deserts can also be cold, wet places. For example, the border between Iraq and Saudi Arabia is subject to sleet and snow, fog, rain and low cloud, and these were the conditions some SAS soldiers faced during the Gulf War.

There are other units that train in the desert, such as the Spanish Legion, French Foreign Legion and the US Marine Corps, but the SAS tops the list when it comes to specialist desert training, which is quite different to simply learning conventional desert warfare skills.

Hostile terrain puts great demands on clothing and equipment

How long does an SAS soldier spend training in hostile environments? Because the Regiment takes the view that there is no such thing as a fully trained SAS soldier, individuals spend many weeks and months on training courses throughout their careers. But training to fight in hostile terrain is only one aspect of the SAS's duties. Other skills to be learnt include hostage-rescue, insertion techniques, patrol skills and clandestine amphibious warfare methods. Troopers may be away from Hereford for eight months of every year (though this also includes time spent on operational duties). Therefore, hostile environments training is limited by the other commitments the Regiment has to fulfil.

Other units devote more time to hostile terrain training. Thus, Australian SAS soldiers undertake one or more international exercises each year, plus several exercises in Australia itself. In addition, there are squadron and inter-squadron competitions which usually involve long marches through hostile terrain (apart from the coastal fringe, the whole of Australia could reasonably be described as hostile terrain!).

As can be seen from the above, SAS troopers receive training to fight in all types of terrain.

This sets them apart from the soldiers of other elite units, who do not receive this diversity of training. To perform in hostile environments, though, requires specialist equipment. What does the SAS use, and how does it compare to that used by other units?

Hostile terrain puts great demands on clothing and equipment, and this is a problem the SAS has encountered many times over the years. For example, footwear posed a major problem during the 1959 war in northern Oman. Individual troopers wore standard-issue British Army boots, which had rubber soles. However, the dry and rocky terrain wore them down so much that the screws that held the soles stuck out like football boot studs, and the toecaps were

also worn away. As a result, some of the most important re-supply drops to the men during the campaign were consignments of new boots.

SAS clothing is tailored to the specific type of environment a team is working in. Each type of hostile terrain presents a number of threats to the human body. The desert heat, for example, can cause sunstroke and fluid loss, and so SAS troopers wear clothing that will trap a layer of air between the skin and the clothing, which will help keep the body cool and limit perspiration. Desert wear consists of lightweight cotton trousers, long-sleeved cotton shirts and headgear to prevent sunstroke (these are usually Arab *shemaghs*, which trap cool air underneath and protect the neck).

Because of the temperature variations in the desert, troopers are often forced to take extra clothing with them on operations. During the 1991 Gulf War, for example, the men who

Below: US Marines during the Gulf War, a photograph that conveys the problems of fighting in the desert: heat, sand and dust, and no cover.

crewed the SAS mobile fighting columns that went into Iraq were clothed in Goretex jackets, climbing jumpers, gloves, arctic smocks and woolly hats. This was in response to the arctic-like weather conditions in the region at the time.

Polar regions pose different problems, and one of the biggest is windchill (when the wind and cold combine to produce extremely low temperatures). In these conditions clothing that offers protection against the cold and wind is of paramount importance. The clothes themselves are worn in layers and are loose-fitting. This allows the blood to circulate freely and helps to prevent frostbite (the freezing of body parts). Though the whole body must be covered in polar regions, troopers must be careful not to overheat. If this happens the resultant sweat can freeze – it is always better to be a little cooler in polar regions than run the risk of perspiring.

Ice got into the feed trays of the GPMGs and made them inoperable

SAS clothing for polar regions includes cotton long johns, wool and nylon socks, Royal Marine cotton trousers, Goretex smocks, 'fitzroy' jackets (made from nylon), gloves, and woolly hats or balaclavas. Keeping the feet warm and dry can be very difficult. It is customary to wear wool socks next to the skin and a nylon pair on top. Feet always sweat when active, and because the boots are waterproof the moisture will remain inside the socks. However, the feet remain warm because the heat given off from the body remains inside the boots.

Apart from the standard military dress worn in temperate climates, the Royal Marines equip their men predominantly for operations in arctic terrain. This means thermal underwear, wind-proof smocks and trousers and white oversuits. The US Marine Corps has adopted the Extended Cold Weather Clothing System (ECWCS) for polar regions. This is basically a four-layer clothing system that includes polypropylene underwear, polyester fibre-pile jacket and trousers, a camouflaged hooded parka and over-trousers made of Goretex.

A similar multi-layered system is used for the cold-weather clothing worn by the US

Above: A group of French Foreign Legionnaires make their way through a rain-sodden tropical jungle in French Guiana.

Rangers: long underwear, wool shirt, field jacket and trousers with liners, arctic parka with fur-ruffed hood, over-trousers with liners, and fur-ruffed arctic mittens with wool mitten inserts. The white insulated boots are complemented by the white camouflage of the outer garments.

Soldiers also need to cover up in tropical environments, although here they do so to prevent being scratched, bitten or stung, since wounds can quickly fester in the humid atmosphere). Because of the high temperatures and humidity, fluid loss through sweating is a severe problem, both from a health point of view and because it can rot clothing. An SAS veteran of the campaign in Borneo (1963-66) remembers the conditions: 'The humidity of the jungle is not immediately obvious because the canopy of

trees casts a psychological shadow of coolness. So you think, well, this isn't so bad after all. But then the humidity hits you, and within an hour both your trousers and shirt are saturated with sweat as the body soaks up the rising warmth. The best way I can describe it is being inside a greenhouse which has no lights. The sun can be scorching the tops of the trees, but on the ground the atmosphere is constantly damp.'

Not only did the conditions themselves cause problems, some of the equipment issued was not up to scratch, which added to the discomfort suffered. The veteran continues: 'Canvas boots to allow the feet to sweat were issued, but early designs suffered due to the poor quality of the material. Some blokes used their initiative and got cobblers in Singapore, who could make you a pair of shoes in half an hour, to stitch a piece of soft leather to their DMS (Direct Moulded Sole) boots. Others had bartered to acquire the more professional-looking US and Australian jungle boots, which had a hard rubber sole with breathable strong uppers.'

SAS jungle clothing consists of loose, baggy trousers, cotton long-sleeved shirts and jungle hats. This style of dress is followed by other elite units. Australian SAS troopers, for example, are equipped with lightweight, loose-fitting jungle/desert camouflage suits. Hard-wearing and quick-drying, they are ideally suited to the tropical and arid regions the unit operates in.

The Special Air Service has learnt many lessons the hard way about what to wear in hostile environments: often its men have gone to a specific region in standard-issue uniform and customised it and adapted other equipment as and when the need arose. The introduction of new materials, such as Goretex, has obviously made the business of fighting in inhospitable terrain much easier, because these materials are light, offer the wearer protection and are comfortable to wear. In truth, the hostile terrain

Above: Dutch Marines in snow-clad mountains, a photograph that conveys the threats to life this environment poses: ice, snow and steep rock faces.

clothing worn by elite units the world over is very similar.

Training and clothing prepare a unit for hostile terrains, but it is actual operations that are the acid test of effectiveness. Sometimes, however, the environment will be too hostile to allow a team to carry out a mission, whatever its dress. An example of this is the SAS debacle on Fortuna Glacier during the Falklands War.

Fortuna Glacier is on the island of South Georgia, and the British plan to retake it from the Argentinians in 1982 was codenamed 'Para-quet'. How to capture the island prompted a fierce debate within the task force detailed to carry it out. The first crack was allotted to Major Cedric Delves, commander of D Squadron, 22 SAS, who decided to land the squadron's Mountain Troop, commanded by Captain John Hamilton, by helicopter on Fortuna Glacier and then move on foot to establish a number of observation posts (OPs) around Leith and Gryt-viken, the main enemy positions, as a preliminary to the main assault. On 21 April 1982, the men were landed on the glacier. This was

extremely ambitious. Indeed, some members of the British Antarctic Survey Team aboard *Endurance* argued that the glacier was impassable due to the weather and the multitude of crevasses. As it turned out, they were right.

Though they had climbing equipment, lightweight sleeping bags, extra warm clothing and bivi-bags, the men were not prepared for the ferocity of the terrain or the weather on the glacier. As soon as they left the Wessex heli-copters they were buffeted by high winds that blew snow into their faces and equipment (ice got into the feed trays of the GPMGs and made the weapons inoperable). The 16-man troop formed a wedge-shaped formation and headed towards their destination. However, their progress was slow, and after five hours of being lashed by wind and snow and pulling heavy sleds, they were forced to make camp in a semi-sheltered spot, having travelled only a few hundred metres. The troop had two small tents, but one blew away in the wind and so the men were forced to take it in turns sleeping inside the one remaining. They were subjected to a Force 11 wind, and it was clear that the men had to be evacuated if their lives were to be saved. From then on it was a race against time to prevent fatalities from hypothermia and loss of limbs through frostbite.

The operation had been just too ambitious, and the SAS had underestimated the weather conditions. Marching through snow and ice is extremely taxing, even with skis and snow shoes, but to do it in a blizzard saps individuals' stamina dramatically. They camped in a spot which offered little shelter, and they had no opportunities to eat a warm meal and get a hot drink: with hindsight, disaster seemed inevitable.

SAS soldiers laid for days, even weeks, in cold, wet hides

Though Fortuna Glacier was a failure, the Regiment went on to take an active part in the retaking of South Georgia and carried out invaluable intelligence-gathering work on the Falkland Islands themselves. This venture involved digging OPs in the peat earth and lying still during daylight hours. Though the hides were lined with thick plastic, the wet inevitably seeped in and soaked the men and their equipment. It was then that the self-discipline of the individual SAS soldier came into play, for no matter how much sophisticated clothing and equipment one has, ultimately willpower is the determining factor and the difference between success and failure. SAS soldiers laid for days, even weeks, in cold, wet hides, recording enemy movements, and eating only one hot meal a day (see Behind the Lines Chapter).

The Regiment has had more success in the jungles of the Far East. The SAS first operated in this terrain during its campaign in Malaya (1948-60). Though actions involving the Malayan Scouts (the predecessors of 22 SAS) were not always successful, by the end of the war against the Malayan Races Liberation Army insurgents the Regiment had all but mastered the art of jungle warfare (the SAS established a jungle

warfare school at Kota Tinggi in Malaya). Tactics involved three- and four-man teams going on extended operations, often for months at a time, deep into the jungle. During these forays the men would move slowly through the dark and damp of the jungle, keeping an eye out for enemy activity. They were always soaked with sweat or rain, and they often ate food cold for fear of lighting fires that might alert the opposition to their presence.

Access to the plateau is via narrow passes, which are ideal for ambushes

In Borneo (1963-66), when the Regiment fought a highly successful campaign against communist insurgents and Indonesian Army regulars, the SAS employed their tried and tested tactic of operating in small patrols, though at first the British commanders wished to use 22 SAS as a mobile reserve, which would be dropped by parachute onto the jungle canopy to recapture areas taken by the Indonesians. The commander of the Regiment at that time, Lieutenant-Colonel John Woodhouse, was horrified, believing that this would result in high casualties. Finally commanders allowed Woodhouse to deploy his SAS men in small patrols along the border, where they could gather intelligence concerning enemy movements. The first unit to be deployed to Borneo was A Squadron, which arrived in early 1963. Though it numbered only 70 men, Woodhouse, by splitting it into two- or three-man patrols, was able to field 21 patrols along the entire length of the border (some 1500km). In addition, the patrols stayed in the jungle for long periods, sometimes up to six months at a time.

What about other units' successes in hostile terrain? They certainly compare favourably with those of the SAS: the Australian SAS triumphs in Borneo and Vietnam (see above), the taking of the Pointe du Hoc on D-Day by the US 2nd Ranger Battalion, and the campaigns by the French Foreign Legion in North Africa in the nineteenth and twentieth centuries are just a handful of spectacular victories in difficult terrain. But what does fighting in hostile environments involve for the men of elite units?

As an illustration of the difficulties elite units face when tackling hostile terrain operations, we may compare the Special Air Service assault on the Jebel Akhdar in Oman in 1959 with Spetsnaz operations in Afghanistan during the Soviet occupation of the country in the 1980s.

The conditions on the jebel required a new set of survival skills

The Jebel Akhdar, or Green Mountain, in the north of Oman consists of an imposing 350-square-kilometre plateau with an area of surrounded by high mountain peaks. Access to the plateau is via narrow passes, which are ideal for ambushes. In the late 1950s, the area was the scene of an uprising against the Sultan of Muscat and Oman. The sultan had a treaty with the British, and they found themselves reluctantly drawn into the conflict. The sultan's rule was being challenged by Suleiman bin Himyar, chief of the Bani Riyam tribe, the Imam, Ghalib bin Ali, and Ghalib's brother, Talib. They had declared the region independent of the sultan and he, having inadequate resources, had turned to the British for help. Conventional forces succeeded in pushing back the rebels onto the jebel, but subsequent attempts to dislodge them failed. Thus, in November 1958, 70 men from D Squadron, 22 SAS, arrived in Oman under the command of Major Johnny Watts.

The men had been previously deployed in the Malayan jungle, and so a period of retraining and acclimatisation to mountain operations was needed, as an SAS corporal relates: 'We set up a series of hard marches with bergens, weapons and ammunition, and at the end of each march there was more and more range work, more and more open work, as opposed to work which we'd always done in jungle, and longer range marksmanship, well over the 25 or 30yds which we had previously engaged in.'

The conditions on the jebel required a new set of survival and operational skills. The rock of the jebel is hard and metallic, which makes silent movement extremely difficult (the SAS troopers initially wore nail-shod boots that generated a lot of noise). Deep-sided ravines slice their way through the plateau, and so SAS patrols had to spend many hours climbing and descending the sheer, rocky faces.

Living off the land was impossible, so SAS patrols had to carry all their rations and equipment with them, including climbing ropes to negotiate difficult terrain. Each SAS soldier could be weighed down with as much as 55kg of kit, which made marches over steep terrain exhausting. Then there was the weather: the climate on the jebel alternated between sub-zero conditions at night and scorching heat during the day. Major Johnny Cooper, an SAS veteran of World War II, remembers the environment well: 'We had arctic sleeping bags, cold and wet weather equipment. It was really freezing. There was rain, freezing sleet, snow – it was horrible.' Afghanistan is very similar in climate to the Jebel Akhdar, with hot, dry summers and dry, cold winters. The snow that falls between November and mid-March makes travel difficult. The geography of the country, too, bears a resemblance to northern Oman: the mountains of the Hindu Kush present a series of formidable barriers to military operations.

Spetsnaz troops had been employed in Afghanistan from day one

The Red Army found this to its cost after it had invaded the country in the winter of 1979. The urban and low-lying areas were quickly subdued, but the mountains became the strongholds of the Mujahedeen rebels. These were ill-equipped and often in fragmented groups, but they could still conduct hit-and-run actions before withdrawing to their mountain hideouts. At first the Soviets tried to deal with them by employing large sweeps of the countryside with tanks, motorised infantry, helicopters, artillery and aircraft. This would result in the Mujahedeen being driven out of the area, at the cost of heavy Russian and Afghan government casualties, but they would return as soon as the Soviets had left. It soon became clear that the way to deal with the Mujahedeen effectively was to pursue them into their mountain hideouts. These small-scale operations were conducted by Spetsnaz units.

In fact, Spetsnaz had been deployed in Afghanistan from day one of the occupation –

Above: An SAS patrol using rafts in Malaya in the early 1950s. The picture illustrates the main drawback to river travel: the risk of ambush.

they assisted in the assault on the heavily defended presidential Darulaman Palace. The commander of the assault, Colonel Boyarinov, ordered that no one was to leave the building alive; in the subsequent firefight he was shot dead by his own men as he left the palace to get reinforcements! Spetsnaz also secured key roads and Kabul airport – but they then spent the first two years of the war defending their barracks and major installations. However, from 1984 there was a shift in emphasis in Soviet tactics in response to the large-scale losses they were suffering, especially in their vehicle convoys. Red Army commanders decided to take the war to the enemy, specifically into those areas where the Mujahedeen had previously felt secure. Spearheading these drives were elite Spetsnaz units.

Above: SAS soldiers being briefed prior to the Jebel Akhdar operation, January 1959. The subsequent attack combined deception and audacity superbly.

Spetsnaz troops sometimes operated in units of two basic sizes – larger groups of 40-50 and smaller reinforced groups of around 18 men that included a forward air controller and an artillery observation officer, two key personnel who could call upon a large amount of firepower if need be. Spetsnaz units were most active on Thursdays and Fridays – the Moslem Holy days – because there was more of a chance that enemy guards would be off duty. The teams would often work with Afghan militia and motorised regiments and divisions, and could spend up to a week or more in the mountains. Like the SAS, they could not live off the land in the barren terrain, so they were dependent on helicopter drops for food, water and ammunition. The main revolution in tactics in Afghanistan was that Spetsnaz troops were trained to think on their own and make autonomous decisions without having to refer to higher command levels – a major step away from the normal rigidity of Red Army doctrine.

These very qualities of initiative and being able to think on their feet are among the characteristics that distinguish SAS soldiers from their conventional counterparts, and they had secured some operational successes in northern Oman by January 1959. For example, two troops under Captain Rory Walker had deployed on the north side of the jebel and established sangers (defensive positions consisting of rock circles) on the heights of Rub' al Khali, only 300m from rebel positions, then held them against subsequent rebel attacks.

It was by no means plain sailing, though. The following is an account by a troop commander of an early reconnaissance undertaken by the SAS on the jebel: 'We got to the top and we found positions that the enemy had obviously occupied, so we decided to get into their positions rather than make new ones of our own, because we knew enough about them to realise that they would spot a new position on the skyline the same as we would if it was our area.

At about 0639 hours the sun came up and we fried and fried and fried. We had two extremes. At night it was cold enough on top of the mountain to freeze the water bottle, and we weren't as well equipped then as we are today. All we had were OG trousers and jacket and a very thin standard issue pullover. We didn't take sleeping bags on a 24-hour recce since all they did was slow you down, and anyway, we didn't intend to sleep, not knowing whether they had established night picquets.

'Around about 1400 hours I had another three men with me in my patrol and we were looking down and covering an area when, lo and behold, I saw this Arab start making his way up.

Below: Lieutenant-Colonel Tony Deane-Drummond, commander of 22 SAS, photographed on the Jebel Akhdar, February 1959.

He got to within 300yds of us when he must have spotted some sort of movement because he shouted up at me, obviously thinking I was one of them. So we shouted down, but then he decided, having had his rifle on his shoulder in the sling position, that something wasn't quite right here, so he took it off whereupon I shot him. My mate alongside me shot him as well and we just blew him away. Within 30 seconds we were under fire from numerous places. They were hyperactive and their reaction was perfect and they started shooting from all areas and concentrating on us. Further along the ridge, the other half of our troop was trapped.'

'In the SAS you always have to see the humour of things'

Daylight reconnaissances were too dangerous because of the fierce heat and the high chance of being spotted and overwhelmed by numerically superior forces. An SAS veteran relates: 'As dawn light came they had a good look and spotted us [his patrol]. Then a great firefight started and we were in a position where we couldn't move out of the rocks otherwise we'd have been dead. In the SAS you always have to see the humour in things. They knew where we were and they were sending exploratory shots pinging all over the place.' Therefore, SAS patrols confined themselves to night work, a tactic used by Spetsnaz teams in Afghanistan, who were dropped by helicopter at night and then set up ambushes along trails and mountain passes.

Despite SAS successes, the rebels were still firmly entrenched on the Jebel Akhdar at the beginning of 1959, and so A Squadron, 22 SAS, was sent to the area as reinforcements. In January the decision was taken to make a determined push against Talib's forces on the jebel. Aerial reconnaissance had revealed that there was a route up the cliffs between two wadis. The SAS launched a diversionary attack from a village called Tanuf, while the main assault – two SAS squadrons – was directed from the village of Kamah to the east. The ruse worked, and by the early hours of 27 January the SAS was poised to break onto the plateau. The commander of the force, Lieutenant-Colonel

Deane-Drummond, decided to make a dash for the summit. Reducing their loads to just essential weapons and ammunition, the men then made a gruelling 90-minute forced march to the top. Total surprise had been achieved, and the resistance of the rebels was broken.

The operation's only disappointment was that the rebel leaders, Suleiman, Ghalib and Talib escaped down the jebel and made their way to Saudi Arabia. The rest, now leaderless, had little enthusiasm to carry on the fight, and by 5 February the entire jebel was in SAS hands.

Spetsnaz operations in Afghanistan were hampered by the fact that the rebels were dispersed around the country (at least in northern Oman the rebels that were fighting the SAS were all contained in one area, albeit a large one). This meant Spetsnaz had to mount many search and destroy missions, in addition to the convoy protection duties and major sweeps they had to undertake. During the 1985 Kunar offensive to relieve Barikot, for example, Spetsnaz forces were inserted deep into rebel-held areas and were used to seize key points on the hills overlooking the relief column. However, casualties were high on both sides, and the Spetsnaz troops holding defensive positions soon became the target of heavy Mujahedeen attacks.

Spetsnaz troops proved adept at using camouflage and concealment

Although time was saved by using helicopters to drop teams on mountain crests, these operations required expertise in mountain warfare. Once deployed, Spetsnaz groups proved adept at gathering intelligence and setting ambushes without being detected.

Improved Mujahedeen air defences, particularly after the acquisition of Stinger hand-held missiles, meant that Spetsnaz troops could make less use of helicopter transports. Nevertheless, Spetsnaz teams continued to seize targets high in the mountain by night. Like their SAS counterparts, this required Spetsnaz soldiers making climbs with bergens weighing up to 30kg. Other equipment included AK-74 assault rifles, silencers, light mortars and even RPG rocket launchers, all strapped on their backs,

though there was obviously a limit to what individuals could carry when making a climb.

In northern Oman, SAS soldiers could call on the support of RAF ground-attack aircraft and Army mortars for support, with pilots and men on the ground communicating by marker panels. In Afghanistan, Spetsnaz soldiers had rather more sophisticated signals equipment, and could call upon helicopter, aircraft, tank and artillery support. The use of Stingers, however, had a damaging effect on heliborne firepower support for Spetsnaz teams. Hind helicopters, operating in pairs, provided good fire support, particularly against Mujahedeen heavy weapons positions, until Stingers blew them out of the sky.

Just as the SAS proved themselves effective warriors on the high ground, so Spetsnaz mastered mountain warfare techniques. According to one Mujahedeen leader, Abdul Haq, stated, Spetsnaz were 'very good at camouflage, map reading, at finding food from nowhere, they are physically strong and good at reconnaissance'. This high level of physical fitness had

Above: Russian troops in Afghanistan. In the background are the mountains that saw many battles between Spetsnaz and the Mujahedeen.

also been a deciding factor in the Jebel Akhdar campaign. As Johnny Cooper states: 'It had to be done quickly. If you'd sent in a battalion of infantry it would have cost a lot of money. Here, you were sending a small gang. It was an SAS job because we had the ability to carry pack-mule loads and we were all very fit.'

The Jebel Akhdar campaign proved that SAS soldiers could be masters at fighting in hostile terrain. Some 20 years later, Afghanistan was to prove a tough testing ground for the Soviet elite, but Spetsnaz proved equal to the task. What both conflicts proved was that elite units could achieve results if they contained motivated men and were allowed operational flexibility. But at the end of the day, success relies on individuals scaling mountains, tramping over frozen glaciers and crossing deserts to get at the enemy. In this the SAS beats all comers.

BEHIND THE LINES

Operations behind the lines are the speciality of the SAS. Such missions require specialist skills and highly trained soldiers. The rewards can be substantial, but so are the risks. How does the SAS compare with other units that operate behind the lines?

This chapter will assess how the SAS measures up to other elite units that operate behind the lines, including Russia's Spetsnaz, the Australian SAS, Israeli sayeret units (these conduct long-range reconnaissance/-surveillance missions and are used for special forces operations along Israel's borders) and the Special Boat Service (SBS). It will examine the behind-the-lines roles of these units, their tactics, and their equipment to determine which is the best at operating in enemy territory. First, we will examine each unit's role behind the lines.

The SAS's role has remained essentially the same as that devised by the Regiment's founder, David Stirling, over 50 years ago. The SAS is still essentially a long-range reconnaissance unit, whose members are trained to operate in wartime unsupported in small groups behind enemy lines.

The SAS's war-winning potential stems from their ability to stay hidden for long periods in observation posts (OPs). From there they reconnoitre enemy installations and movements, and then send this information back to headquarters via long-range communications equipment.

You're a long way from the water. While two of his companions survey the horizon, a US Navy SEAL keeps watch for enemy soldiers during an operation behind enemy lines.

Above: A heavily armed SAS jeep patrol behind German lines in France during Operation 'Houndsworth' in July 1944.

This was the role envisaged for the Regiment, and its Territorial Army counterparts (21 and 23 SAS), in any conflict in Europe between NATO and the Warsaw Pact.

In a large-scale conventional war, the Regiment would be fully committed to gathering intelligence, but where circumstances permit SAS teams could also undertake more aggressive actions in enemy rear areas. Operating behind the lines in northwest Europe in 1944-45 with assistance from local resistance groups, for example, SAS teams killed or wounded nearly 8000 German soldiers and captured a further 4784; destroyed 700 enemy vehicles, seven trains (derailing a further 33); and cut railway lines on 164 occasions. They also reported a host of bombing targets to the RAF and relayed intelligence back to England. How does this compare to the roles performed by other elite units behind the lines?

Australian SAS operations would begin with teams mounting deep- and medium-penetration reconnaissance and surveillance missions on the enemy's flanks and rear to collect intelligence which cannot be acquired by conventional units. Then Australian SAS patrols would mount harassing operations to weaken the enemy's main effort by cutting his lines of communication using ambushes, sabotage and designating targets for air strikes. In addition, raids would be mounted against base areas and specialist targets: headquarters, helicopter bases and supply dumps (if parts of Australia are overrun in a future conflict, SAS patrols would operate in the stay-behind role). Third, teams would mount operations behind enemy lines to retrieve selected POWs, VIPs, sensitive equipment and important documents.

Russia's Spetsnaz warriors take a more offensive role than their Western counterparts when operating behind enemy lines. In any conflict initiated by Russia, Spetsnaz teams would be tasked with performing a number of functions that are important to overall Russian objectives. These tasks include knocking out enemy nuclear weapons and their associated command centres by direct action or by targeting air or artillery strikes; destroying bridges, roads and springing ambushes to disrupt the enemy's chain of command; depleting enemy air assets by destroying operations centres, early warning radars, support facilities, and assassinating pilots; assassinating key enemy military personnel; seizing or destroying important targets, such as power stations; and gathering intelligence through captured documents or personnel.

Spetsnaz must always have a large number of troops available if all their mission objectives are to be accomplished, not least to compensate for the high rate of attrition of Spetsnaz personnel trying to reach their objectives. This rate is certainly far higher than that for units such as the British SAS. As a consequence, Russia currently has five Spetsnaz brigades, each one numbering around 1400 men.

Another formation that maintains large numbers of soldiers for operations behind enemy lines is the North Korean Special Purpose Corps, whose members are trained in infiltration, intelligence gathering, sabotage, underwater demolition and unarmed combat. Political indoctrination accompanies this training, and there are teams of assassins under the control of a branch of North Korea's foreign intelligence service.

South Africa's Reconnaissance Commandos specialised in operations deep inside enemy territory, specifically striking at black guerrilla camps inside the so-called 'Front Line States'. Operating in small teams for long periods in hostile territory, individual commandos needed to be adaptable, disciplined, proficient in weapons handling, have good powers of observation, have good reflexes, and be able to cope with stress. Some commando units operated up to 3000km inside enemy territory, collecting information on guerrilla camps for subsequent air strikes and raids.

Below: An Iraqi target explodes after being hit by UN bombs during the 1991 Gulf War. Targeting courtesy of Britain's Special Air Service.

The Reconnaissance Commandos were employed in Angola and elsewhere in the late 1970s and early 1980s in a series of operations against the South West African People's Organisation (SWAPO), a black guerrilla group dedicated to the liberation of South African-occupied Namibia. These operations were invariably clandestine and employed hit-and-run tactics. On protracted missions the commandos used the bases of conventional units stationed on the frontline, but for short-lived operations they were parachuted into the target area and made their own way back to base. Among the more notable missions undertaken by the commandos were Operation 'Saffron' in August 1979, in which South African forces mounted a reprisal raid into southwest Zambia; Operation 'Mebos' (July-August 1982), in which SWAPO's Eastern Front HQ in Angola was destroyed by a lightning strike mounted by the Commandos; and Operation 'Askari' (December 1983-January 1984), in which a pre-emptive South African raid into Angola severely disrupted SWAPO's logistics and organisation.

Elite soldiers often have to cover long distances on foot

What are the qualities required for operations behind the lines? Physical fitness is a major requirement, allied of course to mental stamina. Elite soldiers often have to cover long distances on foot, since they may be dropped off many kilometres from their objective to reduce the possibility of being discovered. Marches are often undertaken at night, and each man can be carrying around 60kg (though in the 1991 Gulf War SAS soldiers were reportedly carrying up to 95kg). All members of the team must be highly trained in insertion techniques, and have in-depth knowledge of enemy equipment and units to collect accurate intelligence.

SAS training ensures that men are adequately prepared for these missions, with regard to both physical fitness and expertise in insertion techniques: by land, sea or air (see Selection and Training Chapter). In addition, the Regiment ensures that its men are thoroughly briefed prior to missions. Its Operations Planning and Intelligence Cell, nicknamed the 'Kremlin', located at Stirling Lines, is responsible for the collation of intelligence and its dissemination to SAS planners. This information includes details of every aspect of the prospective theatre of operations: local geography, political infrastructure, climate, government, police, economy and armed forces – in short, everything that is needed to plan an SAS operation anywhere in the world.

It is likely that the SAS HQ would have to relocate to the bush

Since the qualities required by soldiers engaged in behind-the-lines operations are virtually standard, it comes as no surprise that other elite units set great store by these same qualities. The Australian SAS requires a high level of physical and mental skill, as well as specialised insertion training. Because planners have envisaged an invasion of Australia by a hi-tech army (such as that of Indonesia), the Regiment has had to train in fairly complicated insertion methods. For example, an approach to a maritime target may require high altitude, low opening (HALO) parachuting (see By Air Chapter), expertise in working with inflatable dinghies and diving skills. One scenario in any invasion of Australia involves the armed forces taking to the 'outback' and waging a guerrilla war against the invaders (because the majority of the population lives on the thin strip of land on the east coast, urban areas would be overrun fairly quickly). This being the case, a comprehensive knowledge of combat survival techniques and medical skills is required. It is highly likely that the SAS headquarters would have to relocate to the bush, and in such a situation the Regiment would be facing a long stay in hostile terrain, something it is well trained for.

Methods of insertion into hostile territory will be dealt with later, but in the meantime, once behind enemy lines, how do elite units operate? The standard operating procedures (SOPs) are universal to all elite units. Great care is taken to minimise the risk of discovery. For example, patrols usually move at night to avoid detection by enemy aircraft or helicopters.

Above: Two 'Diggers' on walkabout in the 'outback' – Australian SAS troopers on an exercise simulating operations behind enemy lines.

Patrols will keep clear of ridges to avoid being silhouetted against the skyline. Bridges, roads and tracks are also avoided if possible, because they are almost invariably mined, booby trapped or guarded. All maps carried by team members are not marked or folded in any way that will indicate the target area, and care is taken not to mark the map with soiled fingers, which can also indicate the mission target. In this way, if the map or its owner fall into enemy hands the mission will not be compromised.

Each patrol member will be carrying a back-breaking amount of kit, for re-supply may be difficult once the mission is under way. In the Falklands, for example, SAS soldiers had bergens filled with waterproof and warm clothing (plus spare clothing), rations, communications equipment, mini torches, gloves, woolly hats, sleeping bag and bivi-bag. Before they set off the men are always briefed on weather conditions, drop-off points and known dispersions of enemy forces. In the Falklands such briefings could take up to three hours – nothing was left to chance.

Once on the ground the patrol leaves the landing site as quickly as possible to reduce the risk of discovery. The objective may be far away, so patrol members will have to move fast to be in position before dawn – no mean feat when each man may be carrying over 60kg on his back, plus his belt, webbing and weapon. SAS soldiers have been known to carry even more weight, most of it ammunition. In the Falklands, it was not unusual for individual SAS soldiers to carry three types of ammunition: 9mm for their Browning High Power handguns, 5.56mm for the M16s and 7.62mm for the patrol GPMG. In addition, each man also carried Claymore mines and M72 Light Anti-tank Weapons (LAWs).

Where circumstances permit, teams may operate in vehicles. In the Gulf War, for example, the SAS mounted mobile fighting columns to hunt for Iraqi Scud missiles and other

Left: David Stirling, the founder of the SAS and the man who laid down the principles for special forces operations behind enemy lines.
Right: South African Reconnaissance Commandos, elite soldiers who conducted a series of devastating raids into countries bordering South Africa that were sheltering guerrilla groups.

selection and training programmes ensure that he is more than qualified to assume this responsibility. Larger patrols, such as those which undertook top-secret cross-border raids into Indonesia during the Borneo campaign in the 1960s (so-called 'Claret' Operations), are normally commanded by troop leaders (usually captains) or squadron commanders (majors).

This contrasts sharply with units such as the North Korean Special Purpose Corps and Spetsnaz, which adhere to a rigid command and control system. This deters junior ranks from taking major decisions, which translates into operational inflexibility. Spetsnaz learned the hard way in Afghanistan, and has changed to a limited extent. But old habits die hard, and there is still rigidity in the decision-making process.

The SAS ambushed Indonesian units by moving down tracks and rivers

The amount of time a patrol can spend behind the lines varies, though most operations tend to be long term. In Malaya in the 1950s, for example, one SAS patrol spent 103 consecutive days in the jungle, its only contact with the outside world being by radio communications. In Borneo, too, SAS patrols operated in the jungle for long periods. For example, one patrol from D Squadron stayed in the jungle in the Long Jawi area for six months.

Being expert at moving unseen through enemy territory, the SAS was the ideal unit to mount top-secret 'Claret' Operations into Indonesia in the 1960s (the British government authorised these raids to pre-empt the build-up of enemy forces by striking at the opposition's forward bases). For these missions SAS soldiers were lightly armed and carried a minimum of supplies. They called themselves the 'Tip Toe Boys' because they hit the enemy and then vanished. The SAS ambushed Indonesian units

important targets. As the United Nations had complete mastery of the skies, vehicles could move during the day without danger of being strafed (though Union Jacks were often flown from vehicles and laid on the ground to prevent 'blue on blue' accidents). These SAS columns could be quite large: around 12 four-wheel drive vehicles (Land Rovers and Unimogs) plus motorcycle outriders.

Other units adopt similar tactics behind the lines. The Australian SAS uses Land Rovers for transportation (see By Land Chapter) and Israeli sayeret units often use heavily armed jeeps on operations. South Africa's Reconnaissance Commandos often used horses to transport their men to and from the operational area. Vehicles or animals mean elite teams can substantially increase the supplies they can carry, which means greater operational range.

Once on the ground, teams are very much on their own. Decisions in the British SAS are left to the commander on the spot, because he is in the best position to judge how to approach the target, what to look for and what actions to take. This may mean that major decisions are left to an SAS corporal, though the Regiment's

Above: A member of Israel's elite sayeret reconnaissance units scans the horizon. Beneath the scruffy appearance lies a crack soldier.

by moving down tracks and rivers and setting booby traps. Patrols from A, B and D Squadrons carried out cross-border raids into Indonesia, and succeeded in stopping the Indonesian occupation of Sarawak and Sabah in Borneo.

However, Israel's sayeret units are comparable to the SAS when it comes to stealthy hit-and-run operations. Sayerets Egoz, Mat'kal, Golani, Shaked and Haruv are expert at hitting Arab guerrilla bases in neighbouring states. For example, Operation 'Argaz Bet' in June 1972 involved the kidnapping of five Syrian Military Intelligence officers in southern Lebanon as 'human ransom' for three Israeli pilots being held in Syrian and Egyptian jails. With the support of armoured units, Sayerets Golani and Egoz captured the Syrians after a brief firefight, being released a few weeks later in exchange for the pilots.

The SAS is second to none when it comes to operational flexibility and self-sufficiency behind the lines. But how does the personal kit carried by individual SAS troopers compare with that used in other units?

Equipment carried by SAS patrols behind enemy lines varies according to mission and terrain, but certain types of kit are common to nearly all operations. One of the most important items of kit carried by an SAS soldier is his bergen. The Regiment prefers the 60- or 80-litre external frame type, both of which must accommodate ammunition for personal weapons, water, food and clothing. Other things carried include spare radio batteries, medical packs, explosives, machine gun ammunition and a laser designator (optional). The belt is another important part of SAS equipment because it holds pouches that contain spare magazines, a compass, knife, bivi-bag and survival kit.

American equipment, as used by the Rangers, Delta Force, SEALs and Green Berets, is very similar to that used by the SAS. It includes the All-purpose Lightweight Individual Carrying Equipment (ALICE) bergen, Kevlar helmets, lightweight Battle Dress Uniforms (BDUs) and combat boots. This kit is just as good as that used by SAS soldiers.

The equipment used by Israeli sayeret units for operations behind enemy lines includes Israeli-made load-bearing vests (customised to include nylon ammunition pouches issued to sayeret formations), Kevlar 'anti-terrorist' flak vests and infantry helmets. This is also just as good as that used by the SAS.

Lead scouts were often equipped with semi-automatic shotguns

What of weapons? Weapons are tailored to mission requirements, but reliability and ability to withstand rough handling are at a premium behind the lines. The M16 assault rifle is compact, easy to fire and is the rifle currently favoured by the SAS, Australian and New Zealand SAS and US elite units. The SAS used to use the larger and heavier SLR, which is robust, reliable and can operate effectively under adverse weather conditions. As its bullet was designed for long-range firing, it may seem surprising that it was used by the SAS in Borneo in the 1960s. However, there weren't enough M16s to go round and individuals found the stopping power of the SLR's 7.62mm round comforting – i.e. when an opponent was hit by one he went down and tended to stay down. The 5.56mm round, on the other hand, has less stopping power.

Special Air Service patrols operating in Malaya often equipped the lead scout with a semi-automatic shotgun because of this weapon's ability to spray shot over a wide area at short ranges. In the often poor visibility of the jungle, any weapon that gave such an advantage in close-quarter fighting was a godsend.

The main weapons used by South Africa's Reconnaissance Commandos were the small arms of their adversaries: Soviet AK-47 and AKM assault rifles and RPK machine guns. Their uniforms were a mixture of Libyan, French, Russian, Portuguese, Egyptian, Cuban and Rhodesian camouflage fatigues, which were copies manufactured in South Africa. These were accompanied by black camouflage cream (white commandos disguised themselves as blacks in enemy areas), anti-tracking overshoes or Rhodesian calf-leather boots with neoprene 'low profile' soles, and special forces webbing that contained collapsible water bottle, field stove, field dressing, pencil flares, lighter, wooden spoon, flashlight, survival/fighting knife and ammunition.

The weapons used by the US Green Berets also varies according to region and requirements. During partisan operations each Special Forces Group will frequently use the weapons of the global region to which it is assigned. Many insurgents throughout the world still use Russian or Chinese weapons, most famously the AK-47. These are ideally suited to hot, dusty or wet climates, relatively immune to abuse and very easy to field-strip and clean (significant qualities when teaching weapons skills to locals with little formal education). In addition, local weapons avoid problems with ammunition shortages and their users being identified by the firing signature of an 'unusual' weapon. For its ability to withstand harsh treatment, the AK-47 is a much better weapon than the M16.

Local forces may be trained and equipped with American weapons

In counter-insurgency operations, local forces may be trained and equipped with American weapons and technology, for example the Civilian Irregular Defense Group (CIDG) programme in Vietnam and the Contras in Nicaragua. In the latter case, the counter-insurgents received training from Green Berets, CIA personnel, Cuban exiles and other mercenaries recruited by the CIA. Instruction was in standard American weapons, such as the M16 and M79 grenade launcher.

Sayeret personnel usually carry Israeli standard-issue weapons, such as the Galil assault rifle and FN MAG machine gun, though they have also been known to use the Russian and American small arms that are in the service of their Arab opponents (particularly useful when operating in enemy territory as the enemy can supply ammunition and weapons).

Among the most important items of kit carried by elite units on behind-the-lines operations is communications equipment. Transmission of intelligence and requests for supplies or extraction require signalling equipment that has good range and frequency attributes, as well as being rugged and secure: soldiers must be able to transmit messages in difficult conditions without revealing the location of the set to the enemy. However, there are two main problems with regard to communications equipment. First, emissions can be intercepted by enemy electronic signal monitoring (ESM) systems, which are tuned into the wavelengths of an opponent's transmitters and usually consist of direction-finding equipment. These systems are backed up by powerful signal processors and computer banks containing all known emitter characteristics. Therefore, the enemy can quickly identify and locate the source of radio signals, which is potentially fatal for an SAS team operating from a covert OP. Second, radio is vulnerable to electronic countermeasures (ECM), especially jamming and deception.

Modern communications systems incorporate data entry devices

How can elite forces get round this problem? Security measures can be incorporated into systems to reduce the risk of being jammed or intercepted by the enemy. Encryption devices, for example, make it very difficult for the enemy to decipher what is being said, though encryption takes up greater bandwidth than a non-secure system. Frequency hopping, whereby the radio automatically changes frequency many times a second in a pattern that is known only to the receiver and transmitter, is another method to prevent enemy interception. However, it is not foolproof, because, like all codes, the pattern can eventually be broken.

How to actually transmit data can also be a problem. The most common way of sending a radio message is by voice. However, this has two main disadvantages for special forces teams. First, there is a possibility of misunderstanding, especially if there is a large amount of data to be transmitted. Second, and more importantly,

there is once again the risk of enemy detection. As a consequence, modern systems incorporate data entry devices. These are about the size of a computer keyboard, and consist of a keyboard, a display screen, a data store and a connection to the radio. The data to be transmitted are first fed into the device, which is not at this point connected to the radio. When the operator has fed all the data into the device, he connects it to the radio and sends the transmission in 'burst' form, which is much faster than by voice.

The PRC319 can store up to 20-preset channels in its memory

The US Green Berets are currently equipped with the capable AN/PRC-77, a short-range FM receiver/transmitter, together with the OA-8990/P digital message device group for checking and sending burst transmissions. However, in the 1991 Gulf War, US Special Forces teams were equipped with three radio sets covering the FM (Frequency Modulation), UHF (Ultra-High Frequency) and SATCOM (satellite communication) bands. SATCOM required an LST-5 lightweight satellite terminal and a heavy satellite dish. However, there were obvious major weight disadvantages with carrying three or more transmitters into battle. Now US Special Operations Command (USSOCOM) has opted to invest in a new multi-channel radio called Joint Advanced Special Operations Radio System (JASORS).

The SAS and Special Boat Service (SBS) are currently equipped with the British-made PRC319, a microprocessor-based tactical radio that gives up to five times more transmission power per kilogram than any other portable radio. The set itself consists of four detachable units: a transmitter/receiver, electronic message unit and two antenna tuners. It also has a pocket-sized electronic unit that is removable from the radio for independent operations. The PRC319 can store up to 20 pre-set channels in its electronic memory and can transmit in burst mode. In addition, and most importantly for elite operations, the set can withstand dust, rain, immersion in water and can be dropped by parachute.

Above: The PRC319 communications set, currently in use with both the SAS and SBS. It is designed to withstand rough treatment on operations.

US communications kit is more sophisticated than the PRC319, but such advanced equipment may mean problems for teams fighting behind the lines in terms of reliability and ability to withstand rough treatment.

The SAS has some of the best-trained and best-equipped soldiers, but what is their record behind the lines? Let us compare the SAS in the Falklands with the SBS in the same conflict to see what two top elite units can accomplish.

The 1982 Falklands War gave the SAS and the SBS the opportunity to prove that they were among the best units in the world for behind-the-line operations. The islands themselves, situated some 13,000km from the United Kingdom, have a cool, damp and windy climate and a terrain that is mostly treeless moorland and rocky hills. These conditions posed many dangers for the SAS and SBS teams that were put ashore from the beginning of May, not least the hazard of being discovered by enemy foot patrols and Argentinian aircraft.

The first problem was how to insert the men onto the islands. Insertion by submarine would have been extremely difficult because the waters are comparatively shallow around the Falklands, thus making any submarine that comes in close more detectable from the air. Airborne insertion was a possibility, and there was a plan to drop the whole of G Squadron onto the southern tip of West Falkland from a Hercules transport aircraft, but the plan was shelved as being too ambitious. That left helicopter insertion. This was preferred for two reasons. First, the Sea

King helicopters of 846 Squadron aboard the carrier HMS *Hermes* were ideal for the task. Second, despite the noise and relatively slow speed of the helicopters, the remoteness of the landing zones and the very windy and inhospitable conditions made helicopter insertion an acceptable risk.

SBS teams usually consisted of four men, each team having three main tasks: to report on the strength and location of Argentinian defences, identify suitable landing sites for the main British force, and find a base where the Royal Marines of 3 Commando Brigade could establish a Brigade Maintenance Area.

The first SBS team left *Hermes* on 30 April. In the darkness the Sea King helicopter flew low to avoid the Argentinian radar screen off the north coast of East Falkland (the pilot was equipped with passive night goggles), and headed for the San Carlos area.

The team was equipped with binoculars, telescopes, night sights, weapons, ammunition, food and spare clothing. Once the men had been dropped off they faced long marches to their destination. Night movement was difficult: the rocks and bogs reduced speed to around 250m an hour, and the constant wind and rain made the experience all the more miserable.

Movement during the day was too risky, and so the men were forced to dig camouflaged positions in the ground. This entailed cutting out sods and then laying them on chicken wire, scraping out the earth to a depth of half a metre, scattering it over a wide area to ensure their digging wouldn't be obvious to any observers, and then covering the scrapes with the sod-covered chicken wire. The sods and additional hessian strips made the scrapes virtually invisible (each morning before dawn the turf camouflage was replaced so that the OP wouldn't have a 'fading' roof).

One SBS team established an OP overlooking the mutton factory at Ajax Bay, where the Royal Marines intended to establish their

Brigade Maintenance Area. It confirmed that the factory was unoccupied and that it would make an ideal landing point. In the days that followed other teams were flown unseen onto the island to carry out further reconnaissance and intelligence work for the Task Force.

The first SAS men to set foot on the Falklands were from G Squadron. Like their SBS comrades they were transported by Sea King helicopters, and reported back to the Task Force on the day-to-day movements and locations of the 11,000-strong enemy garrison and more than 40 helicopters and aircraft that the Argentinians possessed.

Typical of the type of work undertaken by the SAS was the OP established by Captain Aldwin Wight on East Falkland. His four-man patrol had been landed on the island in early May to report on Argentinian movements around Stanley. The men established a camouflaged OP on Beaver Ridge, which overlooks Stanley. They reported on enemy movements using burst transmissions and pointed out that the enemy had a night dispersal area for helicopters situated between Mount Kent and Mount Estancia. This information resulted in Sea Harriers attacking the site and destroying three of the helicopters. Wight and his men endured 26 days of living in the OP, before being relieved on 25 May.

Movement, talking and cooking during the day was impossible

The conditions inside the OPs were dreadful, the discomfort being added to by the constant threat of discovery. The men were permanently cold and wet, and so if there was a chance of re-supply they always requested thick plastic sheets to line the 'hides'. Movement, talking and cooking during the day was impossible, resulting in aching limbs and frozen bodies. Only at night did the SAS soldiers have a chance to stretch their legs and eat a hot meal. Naturally such living took its toll, and one SAS regular commented that after undertaking OP work, 'some of the fittest men we have, returned weak and looking like old men.'

More recently, the SAS has also operated behind the lines in the former Yugoslavia. Under the direction of Lieutenant-General Sir Michael Rose, UN commander in Bosnia, SAS teams have been active in Serb territory. On 15 March 1994, for example, Rose sent a 10-man SAS team into the Serb-besieged Moslem town of Maglai to assess the situation and locate drop zones for US Air Force food drops. Some SAS men infiltrated Serb lines on foot, while others were flown in by Royal Navy Sea King helicopters. Five days later, a relief force from the Coldstream Guards drove through Serb lines, with SAS forward controllers directing NATO fighters to provide air cover.

A seven-man SAS team was sent through Serb lines

On 6 April, Rose tried a similar operation at another besieged Moslem town – Gorazde. A seven-man SAS team was sent through Serb lines in UN Land Rovers. When the Serbs began to shell UN headquarters in the town, the SAS team requested air strikes. The SAS soldiers used satellite navigation devices to pinpoint their own positions, and then employed laser range finders to find the exact distance to enemy positions. The coordinates were then passed to the pilots of overhead NATO F-16s, which attacked the Serb positions. The SAS team came under heavy Serb fire, and one man, Corporal Fergus Rennie (formerly of The Parachute Regiment), was killed on 15 April. General Rose ordered the SAS team out of Gorazde on 18 April, which involved the men walking 8km through Serb lines at night to reach an evacuation helicopter. The episode illustrates the effectiveness of small-sized teams operating in enemy territory and relaying back information, but also points to the dangers such missions involve.

So who is the best? Consider this fact: during the 1991 Gulf War there were over 300 SAS soldiers deployed, with most of them operating behind Iraqi lines for a period of several weeks, gathering intelligence and hunting for Scud surface-to-surface missiles. The total number of SAS soldiers killed during the whole conflict was four men. There is no other elite unit in the world, past or present, that can claim such a record.

BY LAND

Since World War II road vehicles have played an integral part in elite unit operations. Who has the best military vehicles and how are they used by elite units on operations?

Insertion techniques play an integral role in elite unit operations. Getting to and from the target is an extremely important part of the mission, and so all special forces devote a great deal of time and effort to developing means that will deliver teams to their destination undetected.

This chapter will examine the vehicle requirements, vehicles and vehicle training of the SAS, and will compare them with those of other elite units that use vehicles, such as the French Foreign Legion, Australian SAS and Green Berets, to determine who is leading the way.

David Stirling, the founder of the SAS, insisted from the beginning that SAS soldiers should be able to arrive at their targets by air, land or sea. The first SAS operation, in November 1941, involved a parachute drop in North Africa behind Axis lines in order to attack the enemy airfields at Tmimi and Gazala. However, the men were dropped off target and many were injured when they landed. The mission had to be abandoned. Thereafter, transport to and from the target was provided by the vehicles of the Long Range Desert Group. Then, in July 1942, the SAS began operating with

Shades of David Stirling in North Africa. SAS Mobility Troops are trained in the use of Land Rover vehicles, such as these in use with the British Army. Note the GPMGs.

US-made Willys jeeps which were used with great success behind the lines against enemy airfields in North Africa.

Ever since World War II, the Regiment has maintained an association with light vehicles, and today each SAS Sabre Squadron has a Mobility Troop that specialises in all aspects of the use of elite unit vehicles: Land Rovers, dune buggy-type vehicles and motorcycles. But what are vehicle requirements with regard to special forces' landborne insertion techniques?

Elite units require vehicles that can operate in any terrain and weather conditions. For manufacturers this can be a daunting task: to build a vehicle that can operate in conditions that range from intense heat, where sand and dust can have a corrosive effect, to temperatures so low that grease and petrol freezes solid. In reality, the most likely environments where special forces will employ wheeled and tracked vehicles is desert and open grassland (teams are usually limited in snow, jungle and mountain terrain to foot travel, with helicopters and aircraft being used for long-distance insertion). However, in the desert there are still

Above: Long Range Desert Group trucks in North Africa in World War II. They were often used to transport SAS teams to their targets.

temperature extremes: intense heat during the day and sub-zero temperatures at night.

Units such as the SAS, Australian SAS and Green Berets, which often operate behind the lines in small groups, require light vehicles that are reliable, can take a lot of punishment and can move at high speed if need be. In addition, they must also be capable of carrying an array of weapons. Many of these requirements are conflicting, and inevitably a compromise has to be reached, because it is impossible for a light vehicle to have high speed and high payload capacity. As elite patrols have to carry all their food, ammunition, water and fuel to support long-range missions, payload capacity is an important part of the equation.

Ideally then, SAS landborne operations, other than those conducted on foot, require vehicles that have relatively high mobility, range, payload characteristics and firepower, though the latter quality isn't absolutely crucial because

SAS teams are not expected to hold ground. For them, vehicle-mounted firepower is for engaging targets of opportunity or for covering a rapid withdrawal in the face of superior odds. As SAS vehicles invariably operate behind enemy lines, they are therefore far away from friendly depots and bases. To support these independent operations over long distances and in hostile terrain, the vehicles themselves have to be able to carry the necessary quantities of food, ammunition and fuel, as mentioned above. Another way is for supply trucks to accompany SAS light vehicles on operations, as was the practice in North Africa in World War II, when Bedford and Ford trucks accompanied SAS jeeps during operations against enemy airfields. Supplies can also be airlifted to patrols by helicopter or parachute drops, though aerial re-supply depends on aircraft availability, airborne superiority and the possible risks of the SAS mission being compromised.

The Legion is equipped for combat against all but heavy forces

How do these requirements compare with the individual needs of other units? The French Foreign Legion, for example, is a part of France's Rapid Action Force (*Force D'Action Rapide*), which is designed mainly for operations in Africa and the Middle East. The deployment of the 6th Light Armoured Division, which is part of the Rapid Action Force, to Saudi Arabia as part of Operation 'Desert Shield' in 1990 is an example. Its role is different to the SAS's.

Containing well-trained troops, the Legion is equipped for combat against all but heavy forces. As such, it has armoured reconnaissance vehicles, armoured cars and light tanks. French Foreign Legion vehicles operate mostly in high-profile roles, such as peacekeeping, and in frontline roles, such as in support of conventional NATO and 'Out of Area' operations. In addition, Legion vehicles have served in countries like Chad to support French interests. Because they are close to logistical support, such roles are quite different from clandestine missions behind enemy lines. Mobility is important, but only as an aid to moving troops

and firepower to seize and hold ground and defeat enemy offensives.

Vehicles now play an important part in US Special Forces doctrine, though surprisingly road vehicles never assumed a major role in doctrine until the 1991 Gulf War. Green Beret teams in wartime infiltrate their operational area by sea or air depending on the availability of transports and the local situation. Their main experience has been in jungle wars, such as Vietnam, where insertion was mainly achieved by helicopter, or indeed on foot.

Australian SAS vehicle groups would remain in stay-behind positions

Although Special Forces Groups are assigned to other parts of the world besides Southeast Asia and Europe, there was never a real belief that they would be called upon to fight in the desert. They had medium-range jeeps and tactics for using them in their operations, but such operations were rare. It was only after Operation 'Eagle Claw' (the abortive attempt to rescue the American hostages being held in Tehran in April 1980) that the Americans began the programme that resulted in the acquisition of the Chenworth Fast Attack Vehicle (see below).

The landborne insertion doctrine for the Australian SAS revolves around the defence of northern Australia against any invasions that may be made by the countries to the north of Australia. In the event of Australia being invaded (it is assumed by the High Command that any invasion will come from the north), Australian SAS vehicle groups would either remain in stay-behind positions (remember that they are already stationed in the potential war zone) or infiltrate themselves behind the lines via the old cattle stock routes that crisscross the area. The mission requirements are simple, aside from trying to interrupt the actual invasion. First, to provide deep reconnaissance and surveillance on the enemy's flanks and rear to provide intelligence that is beyond the range and capabilities of conventional units to acquire. Second, to perform harassing operations to weaken the enemy's main effort by cutting his lines of communication.

Above: A French Foreign Legion wheeled VAB armoured personnel carrier photographed during the 1991 Gulf War.

The elite unit that probably makes the most of vehicle infiltration is the US Rangers. In snow and ice areas Rangers make use of Snow Cats, motorised sledges, skis and snow shoes, but in desert and other flat, open terrain they employ jeeps to mount raids and interdiction missions. In Ranger vehicle-mounted operations the emphasis is on short distances and firepower. The one major problem for the Rangers is getting the vehicles to the operational area (during the US interventions in Grenada and Panama, for example, paratroopers had to seize airfields before the Rangers could land). This means flexibility is limited, and Ranger vehicles are unsuited to long-range covert insertions, as practised by the British SAS.

What vehicles are used by elite units and who has the best? The British SAS has a long association with Land Rover vehicles. The Regiment has traditionally used long-wheelbase versions of Land Rovers because they have a large carrying capacity. The most famous of these was the so-called 'Pink Panther', a Series II 109in chassis model. It had no doors, was equipped with smoke canisters and had a spare wheel mounted over the front bumper. Its name derived from the fact that it was painted pink for desert operations, to blend in with the pink haze frequently seen in the desert. SAS 'Pink Panthers' were eventually used all over the world, but were replaced from the 1980s by the Land Rover One-Ten.

Land Rover One-Tens have many attributes that particularly endear them to SAS units: they have coil-spring suspension similar to that used on the Range Rover; they are powerful and agile at low speed in mud and sand, and relatively fast on roads; they have excellent power-to-weight ratios and good underbelly clearance; their even weight distribution means they are effective on soft surfaces, and their reliability is excellent. Land Rover aluminium bodywork can take a lot of punishment, and routine field maintenance can be carried out with a panel hammer if need be – useful when you are hundreds of kilometres from a depot.

SAS jeeps during World War II traditionally mounted considerable firepower, and today's Land Rovers carry on this tradition. During the 1991 Gulf War, for example, SAS Land Rovers were armed with varied combinations of Browning machine guns, GPMGs, Mark 19 40mm automatic grenade launchers, Milan anti-tank missiles and Stinger surface-to-air missiles. Such firepower came in handy during operations in the Gulf (see below).

The Land Rover Special Operations Vehicle (SOV) is a larger vehicle built for SAS operations. Capable of carrying a crew of six (One-tens in the Gulf usually had a crew of three), the SOV carries machine guns front and rear (in addition to the twin mounts on the pulpit), an 81mm mortar, a 51mm mortar and mounts for personal weapons. In addition, Milan or TOW (Tube-launched, Optically tracked,

Wire-guided) anti-tank missile or a 30mm cannon can be mounted on the pulpit instead of the twin machine guns if required. How do the vehicles of other units compare?

Like its British counterpart, the Australian SAS uses the long-wheelbased Land Rover, because it is one of the few vehicles that can cope with the large distances involved, the amount of kit to be carried and the need to service the vehicles under operational conditions. The Land Rover has been tried and tested in these areas, and not just by the military: farmers and explorers also appreciate its attributes.

Until quite recently, the US Rangers employed so-called 'gun jeeps' for their vehicle operations. These were Ford M151 utility trucks that were armed with a variety of weapons, including two 7.62mm M60 machine guns,

Below: Mobile fury: a French ERC-90 reconnaissance vehicle, which can reach targets quickly and packs a punch with its 90mm main gun.

Above: The famous SAS 'Pink Panther', a Land Rover Series II long-range desert patrol vehicle. The colour blends in with the desert.

90mm M67 recoilless rifles, M72 Light Anti-tank Weapons (LAWs) and Claymore anti-personnel mines. They were potent short-range weapons platforms, but lacked the range and durability of SAS Land Rovers. The replacement for the M151 is the High Mobility Multipurpose Wheeled Vehicle (HMMWV), which is designed to operate in all types of terrain and climate. Through the use of common components and kits it can be turned into a number of variants, including a cargo/troop carrier, armament carrier, ambulance or TOW missile carrier. It is more versatile than the Land Rover, though the latter has greater range.

Many of the vehicles of the French Foreign Legion are not directly comparable to those of the SAS, being conventional armoured personnel carriers or armoured cars. However, they are also used as highly mobile firepower platforms, as per SAS vehicles. The Legion uses VLR and AML armoured cars in the reconnaissance-/cavalry role. French armoured cars have traditionally been heavily armed. The AML-90, for example, a four-wheeled vehicle, has a 90mm smoothbore gun. Though not normally amphibious, it can be equipped with a flotation screen and propelled through still water by tyre action.

A fully amphibious vehicle in Legion service is the Renault VAB 4x4 wheeled armoured personnel carrier. The steel hull is divided into a crew compartment in front, an engine compartment in the centre and a troop compartment in the rear that can carry up to ten soldiers. Though the VAB is normally armed with only one 7.62mm machine gun, the Legion's cavalry regiment, 1st REC (*Régiment Etranger de Cavalerie*), uses a version that is equipped with HOT anti-tank missiles (a wire-guided anti-tank

Above: An Australian SAS long-wheelbase Land Rover desert patrol vehicle – ideally suited to the rugged terrain of the 'outback'.

missile capable of penetrating 1.27m of armour). Another vehicle in use with 1st REC is the AMX-10RC tank destroyer, a derivative of the AMX-10 infantry fighting vehicle.

The Legion uses its armoured cars and fighting vehicles according to French military doctrine: for scouting and screening, and with the armoured cars being used for raids, for striking at the flanks of enemy penetrations or for hitting supply routes. Their 90mm and 105mm guns can hold their own at long ranges against other armoured vehicles, but the vehicles are vulnerable to faster and lighter vehicles armed with quick-firing weapons.

In comparison, the paratroopers of the 2nd REP are equipped with vehicles similar to those used by the SAS: heavily armed jeeps mounting machine guns and Milan anti-tank missiles – just the sort of combination that could be lethal to the heavier and slower armoured cars and tank destroyers used by their 1st REC colleagues. However, like US light vehicles, they lack the range of the Land Rover.

With regard to jeep-type vehicles, it can be seen that the Land Rovers used by the SAS allow the unit a wide degree of flexibility with regard to range, payload and firepower. US and French vehicles may pack more punch, but they are limited when it comes to range and payload.

One of the most interesting developments in vehicles and their use by elite units has taken place in America. The US Army undertook initial work on the feasibility of establishing a battalion equipped with light attack/reconnaissance vehicles. The only vehicle to complete all the subsequent tests successfully was the Chenworth Fast Attack Vehicle (FAV), which was used by the Americans during the Gulf War.

Above: The Land Rover Special Operations Vehicle, complete with anti-tank and anti-aircraft weapons. A potent mobile firing platform.

The FAV has a number of attributes that make it ideal for clandestine work: it can accelerate to a speed of 48km/hr in less than six seconds when carrying a 640kg payload, climb 60 per cent slopes and operate on 40 per cent side slopes. It can ford up to 45cm of water without modification, and has an unrefuelled range of 528km. If this seems large, though, remember that the distances covered can be immense: during World War II, for example, SAS patrols in North Africa were operating in an area approximately the size of India. The roles envisaged by the US Army for the FAV included command and control, weapons carriage, rear-area operations, reconnaissance, forward observation and laser designation for artillery and naval gunfire. None of these roles were lang-range, though.

The adoption of the FAV by the Green Berets was revolutionary doctrinally. In contrast, the changes to SAS vehicles have come more slowly, by evolution. The SAS used heavily armed and equipped jeeps in World War II, and then progressed to Land Rovers from the early 1960s. But the basic component remained the same: a light vehicle with a crew of two or three that was armed with around three machine guns and carried as much fuel, water, ammunition and food as possible. The Land Rovers in the Gulf also carried anti-tank and anti-aircraft missiles, but the lineage was there for all to see. If anything, with the SOV the trend in the Regiment is towards slightly larger vehicles that can pack a bigger 'punch'. However, the FAV and similar models signal a new direction in special forces land operations techniques.

When operating in enemy territory, FAV-like vehicles have a number of distinct advantages: they are easier to conceal than larger vehicles, both on and off the road; they can use small tracks and access points (gates, bridges, barriers and passes); they can be manhandled by their crews if necessary; and their low silhouettes can reduce radar and thermal signatures.

It would be all but annihilated if subjected to attack by enemy aircraft

The SAS was quick to note developments across the Atlantic, and its own trials with the Longline Light Strike Vehicle (LSV) resulted in a number of them accompanying the Regiment to the Gulf in the autumn of 1990. However, they were used only to reconnoitre the border area – for long-range operations deep into Iraq the Regiment preferred the tried and tested heavily laden Land Rover.

The FAV is a better vehicle than the LSV in terms of range and payload, but both suffer from the limitations associated with military 'dune buggies': their payload capacity is around a third of that of larger vehicles, which limits their operational radius (unless they can be re-supplied); they cannot carry as many weapons as their larger counterparts; overall they are less comfortable for their crews; and they are less reliable than larger vehicles (dune buggies tend to have exposed engines, open to the elements).

When considering the use of vehicles by elite units, there is a further factor to bear in mind, and that is the availability of air transport to take them to and from the theatre of operations. The Australian SAS has no deployment problems with its vehicles, because its training is centred almost entirely around the defence of northern Australia. The men and machines are already 'in theatre' and their landborne mobility is very good and very flexible.

The British SAS also has no such problems transporting its Land Rovers. They can be accommodated within the fuselage of a C-130 Hercules transport aircraft (of which Britain has over 60). The refuelling probes fitted to the aircraft mean that the vehicles can be deployed anywhere in the world, and they can be dropped by parachute if required.

Compared to the SAS, other units have severe problems concerning the deployment of vehicle assets. The French Foreign Legion is one of these. The Legion is attached to France's Rapid Action Force (see above), part of whose remit is interventions in Africa and the Middle East. However, it is limited by the general lack of air, and amphibious, transport capacity. Past operations in Africa have relied on US aircraft and civil airliners commandeered from Air France. During the 1978 intervention in Kolwezi, for example, 2nd REP was transported to the area by chartered civilian aircraft and French Air Force DC-8s. Support elements were flown in by the US Air Force.

The Spanish Legion has no dedicated air assets (or heavy armour or artillery for that matter). This means that its vehicles would have to travel by road in any major conflict. Though its vehicles could undoubtedly reach European operational areas by road, and Morocco is just across the straits of Gibraltar, unsupported it would face considerable difficulties against an enemy formation equipped with tanks. It would be all but annihilated (as would any unprotected vehicle force) if subjected to continuous attack by enemy aircraft (witness German forces in Normandy in the summer of 1944 and Iraqi ground units in the 1991 Gulf War, both of which had no air cover and suffered accordingly).

SAS training exercises in the Middle East are long and arduous

Having vehicles to undertake landborne insertion is one thing, but training men to drive them is another. Training in special operations driving techniques is tough. For British troopers who join SAS Mobility Troops, driving courses begin at Stirling Lines at Hereford, where the Regiment has its own workshops and driving installations. These are then followed by courses at various Royal Corps of Transport and Royal Electrical and Mechanical Engineers establishments in the UK, for example at the School of Army Transport at Beverley in

Humberside. Training then shifts to Middle East countries like Oman and the United Arab Emirates. Training exercises are long and arduous in order to introduce drivers to the wilting effect of the climate and terrain. Subjects taught include the need to avoid the tracks of the preceding vehicle, driving in dune areas, choice of the best ground, selection of proper gear ratios and the capabilities of the vehicles. The drivers are taught to make maximum use of vehicle momentum and gear changes and to avoid sudden acceleration or braking. There are also courses in navigation.

Specialist knowledge is also required to prevent vehicles getting damaged. In sand, for example, vehicle loads must be evenly distributed to prevent sinking into the soft surface; rock-strewn areas cause jolting that wears tracks, wheels, springs and shock absorbers; cactus and thorn bushes cause tyre punctures. These may seem trivial. However, damaged parts need replacing, and this can mean vehicles having to carry spares, which all adds extra weight.

Specialist training for reconnaissance and anti-tank vehicles in the French Foreign Legion is handled by 1st REC, while vehicle training in the Spanish Legion is handled by the various tercios, of which there are four. Vehicle training and combat readiness within the 3rd Tercio ('Don Juan de Austria') are said to be quite high, though the fact that the unit is 'stranded' in the Canary Islands militates against its overall combat effectiveness.

US Special Forces are trained in both vehicle tactics and movement

Unlike 22 SAS, the US Green Berets have no specialist courses in vehicle operation and maintenance. However, Delta Force members must have been given specialist training in maintaining their FAVs before they took them into the Iraqi desert in the 1991 Gulf War. This ad hoc approach reflects the lack of time, money and thought put into vehicle operations by the Americans when compared to the British SAS. On the other hand, the Americans do enjoy a greater range of air support to deploy and re-supply vehicle teams.

US Special Forces, however, are trained in both vehicle tactics and movement, which closely mirror the operating procedures of foot patrols: the front vehicle acts as the lead scout and the convoy moves by alternate bounds. That is, the lead vehicle is halted in a surveillance position to observe the road ahead. While it acts as cover, the second vehicle moves forward, passes the lead vehicle, and then stops in another surveillance position some way forward, being covered all the time by what was the lead vehicle. In this way the column can advance with some protection.

SAS vehicle patrols operate in poorly explored areas

When the Australian SAS left Vietnam (December 1972), long-range surveillance patrols in the vastness of northwestern Australia were assigned a high priority. Some parts of northwestern Australia still remained unexplored and had only ever been mapped by aircraft and satellite. Officers and NCOs were despatched to 22 SAS to be taught desert navigation. They learned solar navigation (using the sun to obtain 'lines of position') and astro-navigation (using the stars for the same purpose). Later came instruction in Global Positioning System (GPS) equipment. GPS makes use of orbiting satellites which transmit precise time and position information 24 hours a day; using receivers GPS users can determine their position anywhere on earth. The Australian SAS also sought out Australian academics who were specialists in navigation and expedition planning to teach these skills to the unit.

Australian vehicle training includes 'outback driving' (negotiating inclines, crossing rivers, winching vehicles over obstacles or out of soft ground); navigation; vehicle service and repair; vehicle tactics (scouting and contact drills); communications and mission planning (fuel requirements, payload priorities, location of checkpoints and lying-up positions); how to locate friendly forces (other surveillance regiments, isolated farms and native encampments with access to fuel caches); and desert survival in summer and winter. During exercises,

Above: TOW-armed US Army HMMWVs take a roadside rest. This versatile vehicle is a replacement for the M151 jeep.

SAS vehicle patrols operating in poorly explored areas survey and map the terrain to provide up-to-date maps in the event of hostilities. Extensive support is provided by Base Squadron's specialists. This contrasts markedly with their British counterpart, which in the 1991 Gulf War against Iraq had to create a temporary squadron – E Squadron – to meet support requirements.

So who's training is best? Despite their resources and numbers, US elite units are light years behind the British and Australian SAS when it comes to vehicle insertion and tactics. For example, the Americans only started to think about vehicles for long-range elite missions in the 1980s. The training in the Spanish and French Legions is basic, and involves no tactics for missions behind the lines. But what of actual vehicle operations?

The 1991 Gulf War affords an excellent comparison between SAS vehicle operations and those of the US Special Forces. UN special forces had been detailed to locate mobile and static Iraqi Scud missile sites for Allied air strikes. The SAS adopted two methods to find the missiles: static road watch patrols and mobile fighting columns. The former were not that successful: South Road Watch abandoned its position straight away because it was untenable, and the men were evacuated by helicopter; Central Road Watch also abandoned its position, the men making a 220km journey to Saudi Arabia; and North Road Watch was discovered and had to make a desperate escape, losing three dead and four captured out of a total of eight. The commander of the North Road Watch had rejected a vehicle-mounted insertion because of lack of cover and fuel. In the light of what happened subsequently, this was a mistake.

The vehicle patrols had more success. The fighting columns comprised 12 or more heavily armed Land Rovers carrying a total of 1.5 tons of supplies, accompanied by motorcycle escorts. Weapons mounted on the Land Rovers included Browning 0.5in heavy machine guns, GPMGs, 40mm automatic grenade launchers, Milan anti-tank missiles and Stinger anti-aircraft missiles (the latter were not necessary as the Allies had complete control of the skies). The columns were drawn from A Squadron (Groups One and Two) and D Squadron (Groups Three and Four). The SAS's operational area ran from Kabala (80km southwest of Baghdad) to Iraq's border with Syria and Jordan. Further north the area was watched by the US Army's Special Forces Delta Force.

The first of the SAS fighting columns crossed the border on 20 January 1991. SAS-identified Scud convoys were identified and attacked by American aircraft on many occasions, though the SAS didn't confine itself to Scuds alone. Other targets included high observation towers, microwave repeater towers and buried fibre-optic cables that enabled Saddam Hussein to communicate with Jordan and his forces in western Iraq.

The SAS quickly established bases, from where they would launch their operations. By the end of January the fighting columns had targeted two Scud convoys for American aircraft and beaten off an attack by an Iraqi company.

On 3 February, an Iraqi column of 14 vehicles was targeted for an air strike, and then raked with SAS Milan missiles and machine-gun fire when it was discovered not all the vehicles had been destroyed. On 5 February, an SAS column designated a Scud convoy for an air strike, shot up an enemy position in a night-time firefight and destroyed an Iraqi observation tower.

The fighting columns were re-supplied by a convoy of 10 four-ton trucks escorted by armed Land Rovers. They carried supplies, vehicle workshops and armourers. The supply column had returned to Allied lines by 17 February, having accomplished its task, by which time a further two Scud convoys had been destroyed.

Though the SAS suffered casualties, including fatalities, they were relatively light. This was due to the total air superiority enjoyed by Allied forces, combined with the elements of speed and surprise used by the SAS. One

Below: The Longline Light Strike Vehicle has seen service with the SAS, but is unlikely to replace the Regiment's Land Rovers.

particularly useful vehicle-mounted weapon was the Milan anti-tank missile, which allowed SAS Land Rovers to engage targets at long range. This meant they didn't have to get too close to the opposition to score a hit.

Meanwhile American Delta Force teams were equipped with armed FAVs, and undertook a role very similar to that of the SAS columns, although Delta operated more in short, penetrating raids than in long-range missions. This was because of the vehicles themselves: the FAVs were not equipped with long-range fuel tanks, which meant they had to stay near base areas. Unlike the SAS, the Americans have little experience of long-range vehicle patrols and no US commander likes to go anywhere without air cover (a doctrine that has persisted since World War II). The FAV was therefore ideally suited to these short-term missions, but depended upon American air assets for re-supply.

The SAS and Delta missions in the Gulf War proved what could be achieved by vehicle columns operating behind enemy lines, but they

Above: The Chenworth Fast Attack Vehicle, as used by US elite teams in the 1991 Gulf War. It packs a powerful punch but has limited range.

also demonstrated the importance of having air superiority over the battlefield (anything on the ground in the desert is a sitting duck). As far as the SAS was concerned, the vehicle column operations in the Gulf were essentially no different from those in North Africa 50 years earlier, apart from the fact that Axis aircraft often attacked vehicle columns in the North African desert (when they did, the men employed a tried and tested SAS tactic: dive for cover). The Americans, on the other hand, were trying something new (they had the luxury of total air superiority to test out their theories). For the SAS it was a case of another opportunity to put well-tried theories into practice. The British SAS, equipped with the excellent Land Rover, proved once again that it is the world's best when it comes to the successful use of vehicles behind the lines.

BY WATER

Landing undetected from the sea is an obvious way for an elite unit to infiltrate enemy territory. Units such as the SAS, SBS and SEALs train their men to do just that.

This chapter will compare the SAS with other maritime elite units – the Special Boat Service (SBS), the Australian SAS, the US Navy SEALs, the Italian COMSUBIN, the French Commando Fusiliers, the US Marine Corps, the Royal Marines, the Russian Naval Infantry and the Israeli Naval Commandos – to determine who has the best-trained and best-equipped. Before any comparisons are made, however, it would be useful to list the wartime roles of the world's main elite maritime units.

True to David Stirling's insistence that SAS soldiers should be able to reach their target by land, sea or air, each Sabre Squadron has a Boat Troop that specialises in all aspects of the use of small boats, canoes, combat swimming and diving. As such, the troops undertake many tasks that are also carried out by the members of Britain's SBS. The essence of the SBS's wartime role is reconnaissance, small raids and sabotage; and the Boat Troops of the SAS also have the skills required to mount such operations. There are only four Boat Troops in the SAS – some 64 men – compared with five squadrons of the SBS. Nevertheless, the SAS's amphibious

Members of Britain's Comacchio Group storm an oilrig during a counter-terrorist exercise in the North Sea. This unit also protects the Royal Navy's nuclear submarines.

specialists make a significant contribution to the efforts of the UK's Special Forces Group.

The popular image of SBS operations is of underwater divers making clandestine raids on enemy shipping moored in harbours and planting limpet mines before stealing away into the night. The destruction of enemy shipping and underwater obstacles is indeed part of the SBS's wartime role, but what does this task actually involve? The truth is less glamourous and more dangerous than imagined.

When they reach the water's edge the scouts may crawl ashore

To destroy shipping in harbours, SBS teams carry equipment and explosives in a buoyancy bag that is partly filled with water to make it weightless underwater (limpet mines can weigh up to 15kg each). Once inside the harbour the divers will use currents to drift from target to target, thereby avoiding creating swirls in the water that may betray their presence to sentries. The precise position in which the mines are placed depends on the type of ship and the configuration of the hull. However, care has to be taken if the boat is preparing to sail, as the divers may be pulled into the propellers or underwater suction openings along the hull.

The reconnaissance of prospective beach landing sites is a major task of maritime special forces, as such information is essential to the success of any subsequent amphibious landings made by conventional forces. Such reconnaissance will identify the slope of the beach, the depth of the water, underwater obstacles, sea conditions and enemy defences. This may involve a hydrographic survey, a beach survey and a surf report. A surf report usually involves a pair of scout swimmers. The swimmers remove their face masks to prevent any reflections off the lenses that may be seen by enemy guards, and record average and maximum wave heights, the length of time between each wave and the angle at which the surf hits the beach. A hydrograpic survey is usually carried out at night and involves scout swimmers, who work in pairs and are kept on course by pairs of guide swimmers. When they reach the water's edge the scouts may crawl

ashore to investigate the composition and gradient of the beach.

The survey will take note of reefs, shoals, currents, kelp and seaweed accumulations, wave patterns and underwater defences. Such knowledge can mean the difference between the success or failure of an amphibious landing. During the Falklands War, a major problem for the British was where to land the ground forces. The islands have a long coastline, so in theory there were many places where troops could have been landed. In practice, however, many of the bays and inlets are treacherous, with kelp reefs and beaches too small to allow the rapid build-up and concentration of ground forces. However, a Royal Marines officer, Major Ewen Southby-Tailyour, had been been stationed on the islands before the Argentinian invasion and had conducted a thorough survey of the coastline in his spare time. As he had been trained as a landing craft officer, he was able to judge the most suitable places for military landing sites, as well as yachting anchorages. By the end of his tour he had amassed 1000 slides and a notebook filled with 100 pages of pencilled notes and sketches. These proved invaluable to the Task Force commanders, who used them to choose the eventual landing site at San Carlos.

One Squadron is tasked with protecting Australian ships and oil rigs

Like its British counterpart, each Australian SAS squadron has a water operations troop, though the unit as a whole is given much wider training in maritime operations than the British. There are several reasons for this. One Squadron is tasked with protecting Australian ships and oil rigs from terrorist attacks, while for Two and Three Squadrons, waterborne operations represent a means to an end. For example, if Indonesia were to threaten New Guinea or the islands under Australian protection, reconnaissance/coast-watching teams might be inserted by water on the many islands in the Flores and Banda Seas to pinpoint Indonesian shipping for attacks by Australian air and naval forces.

Australians are keenly aware that coast-watchers played a key role in the battles around

Above: Special Boat Service divers come ashore during an exercise. Britain's maritime specialists work closely with the SAS.

the Solomon Islands during World War II. Like Japan in that conflict, today's possible aggressors in the region, Indonesia and China, would be faced with an island war before being in a position to strike at the Australian mainland. During the Solomons campaign, teams of Australian coast-watchers with their own boats were able to move from island to island to set up observation posts and avoid Japanese search parties. They also managed to rescue a large

Above: US Navy SEALs prepare to make a 'wet' jump from the rear of a Sea Knight helicopter – a somewhat hazardous tactic.

number of downed aircrew (another current SAS mission). Therefore, any future conflict in the waters north of Australia will require fully trained maritime special forces teams.

The usefulness of SAS teams to combat any future seaborne aggression against Australia was demonstrated during exercise 'Kangaroo II', conducted around Shoalwater Bay, Queensland,

in October 1976. During this exercise, Australian naval and air force assets were unable to penetrate the air and electronic defences of the 'Orange Force' invasion fleet. However, this was solved by placing a small SAS party on an island overlooking the anchorage. Not only did the SAS identify most of the capital ships, but they also successfully acquired a number of 'enemy' vessels for strikes by 'stand-off' missiles.

Maritime special forces have also found a place in the order of battle of other nations. The US Navy, for example, has equivalents to the SAS and SBS in its SEAL teams. The SEALs have three specific maritime missions. First, to provide support for naval operations: this entails beach reconnaissance for assaults or covert landings, reconnaissance of targets (usually close to the beach or waterway), and the elimination of strongpoints and mine clearing, all in support of amphibious landings. Second, counter-terrorism, with an emphasis on maritime situations (SEAL Teams Five and Six work with Delta under US Joint Special Operations Command). Third, maritime operations with other elements of US Joint Special Operations Command.

The Italian Navy's special operations force, *Commando Raggruppamento Subacqui ed Incursori*

(COMSUBIN), is involved in all types of naval special operations and all aspects of maritime unconventional warfare, including reconnaissance and raiding. Another unit that undertakes the full spectrum of elite maritime operations is Israel's Naval Commandos (see below).

France's Marine Commando Fusiliers have three specific maritime roles. First, to handle maritime operations within the new French Special Operations Command. Second, to support the Rapid Action Force as part of the 11th Parachute Division. Third, to support French naval landings.

Physically larger amphibious forces have a wider and more ambitious range of roles. They bear little resemblance to units like the SAS, but their personnel still require specialist training and equipment. The US Marine Corps has an overall manpower strength of 183,000, and it is

Below: Beneath the waves, SEALs practise insertion techniques with a US Navy submarine. The SEALs also use SDVs underwater.

tasked with sustained military missions in support of US forces, amphibious raids, show-of-force operations, deployment of mobile training teams, disaster relief and emergency hostage-rescue operations.

Force Recon Company deploys four-man teams for special operations

A more specialist type of unit within the US Marine Corps are the 'Recons', which are dedicated unconventional warfare forces. Recon units are divided into Force Recon Company and Battalion Recon Company. Force Recon Company deploys four-man teams for a range of special operations: long-range reconnaissance patrols, target acquisition for artillery and naval gunfire, beach reconnaissance, forward aircraft control and raids. All members are highly skilled combat swimmers, parachutists and small boat handlers. As in the SAS, each man is also trained in two or more team specialities: demolitions, signals, medicine and special weapons. Force Recon is tasked by the Landing Force Commander for high-risk strategic missions. Battalion Recon is larger than Force Recon, deploying 500 men in the less specialised role of gathering intelligence about the general area to be used for landings by the parent marine division.

Britain's Royal Marine Commandos (7000 men) are commanded by the Major-General, Royal Marines, through Headquarters Commando Forces, which organises the operations and exercises for UK-based commandos and is responsible for the deployment of 3 Commando Brigade. The latter remains committed to the defence of NATO's Northern Flank in Norway and to providing 'Out of Area' forces to take care of British interests, as well as providing relief and peacekeeping units.

Two of the Marines' three commandos, 42 and 45 Commandos, specialise in cold-weather warfare. In the now unlikely event of war in Norway, the British would be joined by the ACE Mobile Force (a multinational NATO formation based around light infantry for rapid deployment; its purpose is intervention in crises), a US Marine Amphibious Brigade and the Canadian Air-Sea Transportable (CAST) Brigade Group.

Above: Australian SAS troopers sharpen up their canoeing skills off the coast of Western Australia. Their vessel is a two-man Klepper canoe.

In contrast, the major role of 40 Commando is 'Out of Area' operations, and its training is geared towards this role: exercises in the jungles of Brunei and NATO amphibious exercises in Europe and the Caribbean. It can also provide emergency relief operations. In November 1970, for example, 40 Commando conducted relief operations in the flooded coastal areas of Bang-

ladesh. The Marines' air and amphibious capabilities proved invaluable in rescuing groups of survivors trapped by the flood waters and in distributing food to the many communities.

The Royal Marines also has a number of smaller units for specialist missions. Comacchio Group, for example, is based with 45 Commando at Arbroath, and is tasked with internal security. Half the group is responsible for the security of naval bases and Britain's nuclear arsenal, while the other half specialises in the protection of offshore oil rigs. Most of these troops are

graduates of the Close Personal Protection and Close Quarter Battle Courses run by the SBS Counter-Terrorist School at Poole in Dorset.

Another specialist unit is 539 Assault Squadron, which was formed after the Falklands War. Basically a unit that provides a small-boat amphibious capability, it consists of four troops: Raiding Troop with three sections, each equipped with five Rigid Raider boats; Landing Craft Troop with two Landing Craft Utility (LCUs), four Landing Craft Vehicle Personnel (LCVPs), and an Assault Beach Unit (ABU);

Support Troop, which provides mechanical and engineering support; and Headquarters Troop , which provides the squadron with communications, transport and logistical support.

Russia's Naval Infantry is a much larger formation, with a strength of 12,000 men. The formation is tasked with large-scale, first-echelon landings, and clearing and holding the beach for the conventional motor-rifle brigades that make up the second-echelon responsible for securing inland objectives. In addition, it is tasked with protecting naval bases. Despite its size, there are only three underwater special forces brigades in the Naval Infantry.

These, then, are the world's main maritime elite units and their roles. But what equipment do they use, and how does that used by the SAS compare with that of other outfits?

Underwater swimming on military operations is very taxing

Maritime insertion, whether on the surface of the water or below it, requires specialist equipment – i.e. some sort of vessel or underwater breathing equipment. To be suitable for elite units, underwater breathing equipment must fulfil a number of requirements. Open Self-Contained Underwater Breathing Apparatus (SCUBA) gear is noisy, lets a lot of air escape into the water and emits tell-tale bubbles. Therefore, SAS and SBS units use closed circuit systems, such as the Oxymax and Drager Lar V. They are very efficient: they remove the exhaled carbon dioxide and recharge the remaining nitrogen gas with oxygen. This means one cylinder can last up to four hours. The disadvantage with re-breathing equipment is that it is not designed to withstand high pressures and limits the diver to shallow waters. On the other hand, operating in shallow water means avoiding enemy swimmer detection systems, and if the kit fails it is easier to get to the surface. These systems are among the best in the world, though a long-term disadvantage is that re-breathing equipment can cause severe bronchial asthma in divers.

Underwater swimming in military operations is very taxing (a distance of 1.5km is considered feasible for swimmers on missions),

and so swimmer delivery vehicles, which drop the diver as close as possible to the target, have become an important part of underwater equipment for special forces. The Subskimmer, which can operate as a high-speed surface craft or as a submersible, once generated a lot of excitement and was tested by the SBS in Scottish waters. However, it was rejected on the grounds of limited payload and range, which are always the cardinal requirements for UK Special Forces Group vehicles.

The SRC can mount a variety of weapons for use on the surface

A vessel along similar lines that seems set to enter service with the SAS and SBS is the Submersible Recovery Craft (SRC), a fast offshore assault craft designed for special forces use and built by the UK firm Souter Copland Composites. It is powered by twin outboard motors and can cruise on the surface at a speed of 30-45 knots and be quickly transformed into a submersible capable of travelling underwater up to range of 10km at a speed of 2-3 knots. As it has been designed for a wide range of missions – clandestine insertion, anti-drug operations and so on – it can mount a variety of weapons for use on the surface, including machine guns, 30mm cannon and surface-to-surface missiles.

The Submersible Recovery Bag (SRB), also made by Souter, acts as a backup for the SRC and enables teams to refuel and replenish underwater or on the surface. The SRB, anchored at various points, can take an attached payload down to any pre-set depth, hold it there, and then either return it to the surface or let it sink to the bottom.

The US Navy's SEALs also use submersible vehicles. The current American Mark 8 Swimmer Delivery Vehicle (SDV) can carry up to four SEALs, as well as a pilot and co-pilot. Typically around 6-9m long and 600-915mm wide, with a cylindrical, torpedo-like body, SDVs are the descendants of the human torpedoes employed by the Italian and British navies in World War II. Powered by electric motors, most SDVs can maintain speeds of 3-4 knots for several hours, and they can accommodate

Above: A US Marine Corps LVTP-7 armoured amphibious vehicle rolls ashore. These transports can carry up to 21 fully equipped troops.

weapons, mines and other equipment essential to maritime missions. The men sit astride the SDV in their wet suits and breathing apparatus and are transported to their targets. However, the men are forced to travel in a crouched position in a depression along the vessel's hull so as to reduce resistance in the water. This means that after a long journey they are so physically drained that they have to rest on the shore for several hours before they can start their mission.

Both SDV and SRC can be transported to the operational area by submarine, and once they have delivered the men to their destination, can be left on the sea floor or river bottom while the team members complete their mission. On their return, the vehicle can be located by means of an underwater beacon. To get back to the ship the team have to locate a second beacon dropped by the submarine at a prearranged rendezvous, after which a third beacon, on the submarine itself and transmitting on a different frequency, guides the SDV in (this is a safety procedure to prevent the SDV being booby-trapped and then sent back to the submarine). The SRC is certainly better than the SDV, if only because it is less physically exhausting for the troops to use.

Surface vehicles are a faster way of transporting elite teams to the target, but are noisier and are less covert, and therefore generally more vulnerable. However, they require less training and less expensive than submersibles. Fast surface craft in SAS and SBS use include the Gemini rubber inflatable and the Rigid Raider, which have all proved their worth on operations. They are easy to use, compact and can take a lot of punishment. The Gemini is usually powered by an 18- or 40-horsepower outboard engine. It comes in three versions: 12-man, 10-man or eight-man. The Rigid Raider, as used by 539 Assault Squadron, is powered by a high-performance 140-horsepower outboard engine, and is ideal for delivering a small team of up to nine men at speed onto a hostile shore.

The main problem with light surface craft is their vulnerability to heavy seas and their dependence on one or two outboard engines. Special forces teams invariably carry a lot of kit with them on operations, which means a heavy payload for the boat. This puts engines under strain, which increases the likelihood of mechanical failure. If this happens the mission may have to be abandoned.

During the Falklands War, D Squadron, 22 SAS, was tasked with establishing observation posts (OPs) on South Georgia, prior to its recapture by the British. The first attempt, by Mountain Troop, ended in disaster on Fortuna Glacier. Undeterred, the SAS commander, Major Cedric Delves, despatched Boat Troop, led by Captain Tim Burls, to establish OPs on Grass Island to observe the enemy-held settlements of

Leith and Husvik. Five Geminis were prepared, and their outboard motors were taken off and started on test rigs on the deck of HMS *Antrim*.

Each Gemini carried three men, and the omens were favourable when they set off in darkness, in calm water and under a clear sky. However, three of the engines now refused to start, and so the other two craft had to tow the three disabled Geminis. Then a heavy wind blew up which severed the lines of two of the disabled Geminis, blowing them into the night.

Three of the Geminis reached their target. One of the two that were lost was found drifting in the ocean by *Antrim*'s Wessex helicopter, while the occupants of the other were forced to wade ashore at Cape Saunders, the last landfall for thousands of kilometres, from where they were eventually rescued. It was a reminder of how vulnerable small craft are.

A Middle Eastern unit that has traditionally placed heavy emphasis on small surface craft is

Below: Rigid Raiders like these were used by the SAS for the assault that took place in Stanley harbour during the 1982 Falklands War.

Above: Russia's Naval Infantry, a force of impressive size, is largely equipped with obsolete and badly maintained hardware.

Israel's Naval Commandos. Primary delivery has usually been by fast attack craft or submarine (the *Tanin* was used to launch divers for the attack on Alexandria on 5 June 1967). Secondary delivery has been by inflatables followed by an underwater insertion to plant limpet mines. In their previous conflicts, for example, the commandos have attacked Egyptian shipping in harbour with light anti-tank weapons (which do not take kindly to being immersed in water), and they were spotted entering A'ardaqa harbour on 21 October 1973 (thus they were obviously on the surface). During the raid against Port Said (16-17 October 1973), inflatables carried Israeli divers to within several hundred metres of the harbour's defensive nets. There seems little evidence to suggest that they have used canoes or underwater delivery vehicles in their operations.

Nevertheless, canoes have been associated with maritime special forces units since World War II. The reasons are not hard to find: they can be dismantled and dropped by parachute, they can be hauled out of the water and carried overland, and their range is limited only by the stamina of their crews. Easy to manhandle, they are also difficult to spot on radar screens. The two-man Klepper used by the SAS, the SBS and the Australian SAS has a wooden frame and has been in service since the 1950s.

Kleppers were used by 22 SAS in the build-up to the Pebble Island raid in May 1982 during the Falklands War. Before the raid could be mounted, intelligence had to be gathered about enemy strengths and the presence of hostile radar. Therefore, a reconnaissance team from D Squadron's Boat Troop was detailed to gathering the required information. The men were dropped by helicopter on 10 May and had to march across a ridge at the end of the Mare Rock headland, carrying their Klepper canoes and bergens with them. Throughout 11 May they watched Pebble Island, before paddling to it under cover of darkness and undertaking their mission. They confirmed there were several Pucara ground-attack aircraft operating from the airstrip, and that routes to and from the target lacked cover.

A unit that has substantial equipment is France's Marine Commando Fusiliers, whose members are all commando- and parachute-trained. They wear the green beret with a badge bearing a brig, a dagger and the Cross of

Above: The Submersible Recovery Craft allows special forces teams to infiltrate enemy coastlines.

Lorraine. The Commando Fusiliers include the Hubert combat swimmers, comprising 63 men.

French operations put a lot of emphasis on the use of aircraft (Super Frelon helicopters) and submarines for primary delivery. In the past they have relied on inflatables, such as the PB4 Zodiac. During exercises the Hubert Group places beacons and markers for the commandos, conducts reconnaissance and eliminates underwater obstacles; it also often operates with the 2nd REP's *Commandos de Renseignement et de l'Action en Profondeur*. Once these tasks have been accomplished, a raiding force that eliminates radar stations, electronic intelligence facilities and strongpoints, and conducts diversionary actions to mislead the defenders about the location of the actual landing beach. The main landing may involved the 9th Marine Infantry Division, with its armour, mechanised infantry, artillery and anti-tank missiles.

Most landings employ heliborne and seaborne forces

Larger maritime formations can deploy a wider and more impressive range of equipment than small, specialist units such as the SAS. The US Marine Corps, for example, can deploy Marine Expeditionary Forces (MEFs) that comprise helicopters and fixed-wing aircraft, ground combat assets and supporting arms and a Force Service Support Group of engineers and transport assets – in total 48,000 marines, 2600 sailors and all the advanced military technology necessary to make successful opposed landings in enemy-held territory.

American commanders do not like to fight without air cover, and this is reflected in the size of the Marine Corps' air assets: 148 fixed-wing aircraft, including F/A-18 Hornets, AV-8B Harriers and A-6 Intruders, and 152 helicopters, such as the CH-46 Sea Knight, CH-53 Sea Stallion and AH-1 Sea Cobra. The Corps is no longer dependent upon shore bases or airfields: it now derives the full benefit of its short take-off/vertical landing (STOVL) Harriers that have over-the-horizon capabilities.

Amphibious landings are supported by a range of specialised ships whose main task is to land battalions of assault infantry. Most have broad, flat upper decks to accommodate STOVL aircraft or helicopters, and all but the Landing Platform Helicopter (LPH) ships carry landing craft. The LPHs (the Iwo Jima class vessels) are used for vertical assaults with helicopters, while the other ships carry troops, vehicles, tanks and stores, either transferring them to landing craft, as in the case of the Landing Platform Docks (LPDs) and Landing Ship Docks (LSDs), or landing by direct beaching in the case of Landing

Ship Tanks (LSTs). Most landings employ both helicopter-borne forces for vertical envelopment of the beachhead and seaborne forces in landing craft, air-cushioned landing craft or the lightly armoured AAV-7A1 amphibious tractors (Amtrac). The last mentioned will be replaced by the Advanced Assault Vehicle (AAV). The Corps is much better equipped than the SAS, but has to carry out large-scale tasks, such as major amphibious landings.

Russia's Naval Infantry is, at first glance, an impressive fighting formation, having nearly 3000 tanks and other armoured vehicles. However, its equipment is somewhat obsolete: outdated T-55 tanks, PT-76 light reconnaissance tanks and BTR-60 armoured personnel carriers still being in common use. Though it is equipped with ship-to-shore hovercraft and the Polnocny class and Alligator class landing ships, one wonders about Russia's ability to conduct a large-scale amphibious operation, something it has not had to do since World War II. The men who staff the Naval Infantry may be willing, but there are grave doubts as to whether the majority of their ships are even seaworthy. The fact is that the Russian state does not have the resources to even adequately maintain its naval fleets, and this includes the ships and hardware of its Naval Infantry.

Combat diving and canoeing are conducted at Poole

It can be seen from the above that for the tasks it performs the SAS is well served when it comes to maritime resources, and in such items as the SRC has some of the best equipment in the world. But if the SAS has some of the best equipment, how does it compare with other units in terms of training? Maritime operations demand specialist training. Indeed, only adequate training and modern training facilities will ensure that a unit's members are up to scratch – and, of course, more specialised roles require longer and more intense specialist training.

SAS soldiers are taught at SBS training centres, as well as at SEAL training establishments in the United States. Combat diving and canoeing are conducted at Poole, Portsmouth,

Above: SBS swimmer canoeists in Klepper canoes conduct an exercise with limpet mines – a tactic that has changed little since World War II.

and in Horsea Lake near Portsmouth. Communications, demolitions, reconnaissance, observation posts, survival and camouflage are usually taught at Poole and tested on Woodbury Common and Dartmoor. All these skills are brought together on small boat exercises that are conducted on the lochs in the highlands of Scotland. There are also several overseas and NATO exercises each year which involve reconnaissance tasks following waterborne insertions.

SAS Boat Troops are tasked with Maritime Counter Measures, and their training is regularly tested each year in the North Sea in a series of so-called 'purple' exercises. SBS personnel also receive training in counter-terrorism, which incorporates exercises at Poole involving hostage-rescue scenarios on ships and oil rigs.

Maritime operations are just a part of the responsibilities of the SAS, and though they receive intensive and first-class training, it is assumed that of the two British units, it is the SBS that is the more highly trained for missions in and on the water.

The US Navy's SEAL Teams receive comprehensive training in maritime warfare skills. For example, at San Clemente Island students are taught underwater and land demolitions. They are also trained on the range of vehicles that are designed to carry them to their target, such as the SDVs and nuclear submarines that have been converted. These include two Ethan Allen class submarines, the *Thomas A. Edison* and the *Thomas Jefferson*, and two Polaris ships, the *Sam Houston* and the *John Marshall*. There is also two Benjamin Franklin class submarines: the *James K. Polk* and the *Kamehameha*. They are capable of carrying SDVs and SEALs through treacherous tides and currents to the enemy coast. Training focuses on working with the SDVs: navigation by computerised satellite and Doppler navigation systems, and using sonar when underwater to avoid anti-submarine nets and patrol craft.

However, overall maritime training is being reduced now that Teams Five and Six specialise in counter-terrorism and the SEAL wartime role now places emphasis on 'far from the shore' operations. In addition, there is a shortage of SDVs and a shortage of equipment for cold-water operations (closed mini submarines in particular). The latter degrades the SEALs' capacity for arctic operations, and contrasts sharply with the SAS and SBS, who are currently experimenting with heated diving suits for missions in arctic waters. An interesting aside with regard to SEAL training involves SEAL teams making a nuisance of themselves in and around the Russian port of Murmansk; the Russians duly invited the SEALs to take a commercial flight to their country, after which they would be given a conducted tour around the North Cape as guests of the Russian Navy!.

One formation that certainly suffers from a shortage of realistic training is Russia's Naval Infantry. There are no overseas exercises and the regiments spend little time at sea aboard their landing ships. This would seem to suggest that the entire formation is undermanned and under-resourced.

There is a heavy emphasis on night exercises in COMSUBIN

A unit whose training and resources are difficult to fault is Italy's COMSUBIN. As it is a dedicated combat-diver formation, it can devote 100 per cent of its time to maritime training. The offensive arm of the COMSUBIN, the *Incursori*, consists of 200 men divided into logistics and operational cells, the latter being divided into small teams of between two and 12 swimmers. There is heavy emphasis on night exercises in the unit, and friendly vessels moving in and out of Italian ports on the northwest coast are said to provide unsuspecting targets for the swimmers. Exercises are divided into three phases: infiltration, attack (simulated mining and sabotage) and exfiltration. There is also heavy emphasis on live firing exercises on wrecks and de-commissioned ships. Its training must be considered better than that given to SAS soldiers; indeed COMSUBIN has the best overall

training, with the SAS, SBS and Australian SAS – which devotes up to 40 per cent of its training time to maritime training – in second place.

Though trained in maritime operations, SAS soldiers have in fact performed relatively few waterborne missions since the Regiment was created in 1941. This is partly because helicopters have to a large extent replaced boats as the means by which a special forces team can infiltrate a hostile shore. However, the Regiment did mount a seaborne raid during the Falklands conflict, and this will be compared with the raid undertaken by Israeli Naval Commandos in 1969 against the Egyptian radar station on Green Island to illustrate how elite units operate with small boats.

The SAS volunteered to put in a raid from the sea as a diversion

By the middle of June 1982, the battle for the control of East Falkland was almost at an end. On the night of 13/14 June, 2 Para was to assault Wireless Ridge, a few kilometres west of the Falklands' capital, Stanley. To take the pressure off 2 Para, the SAS volunteered to put in a diversionary raid from the sea. The target was a large Argentinian ordnance depot, and the approach was to be by a narrow strip of water immediately to the north of Port Stanley. It was risky, but that is what elite tasks are all about.

In July 1969, at the height of the so-called War of Attrition between Israel and her Arab neighbours, a small team of Israeli Naval Commandos was despatched to destroy the Egyptian radar station on Green Island in the Gulf of Suez (the destruction of the complex was crucial to the success of a series of Israeli air attacks against Egypt). The Naval Commandos were chosen because of their success earlier at Ras el Adabi'a radar station. In that action the Israelis had reached the station by rubber dinghy and had swam the last 100m to the target. The attack itself was superbly executed, with 32 Egyptians killed and all the radars destroyed. What's more, the Israelis had fired only three shots per Egyptian killed, while in similar operations records showed that Israeli para-troopers had unloaded two full magazines of ammunition for each enemy soldier killed. The Naval Commandos were thus more suited.

Green Island itself was well defended: 100 Egyptian soldiers, six emplacements mounting 37mm and 85mm anti-aircraft guns, 14 heavy machine guns and a number of 20mm cannon. Any seaborne force that was spotted on the surface would be quickly blown to pieces. The Naval Commandos were led by Lieutenant-Colonel Zeev Almog, who split his men into three assault teams. Two would attack the radar station while the third provided covering fire. The approach to the target was made in Zodiac inflatables which were powered by outboards. The men wore diving suits and were equipped with breathing apparatus for the final underwater leg of the journey.

There were 8000 Argentinian soldiers in and around Stanley

The Israelis employed two elements in their mission, each of which are essential for the success of small unit operations: surprise and an approach under cover of darkness. The SAS was to do likewise, though there was one major difference between the two raids. Because of the ad hoc nature of the SAS attack, there was little time to thrash out details beforehand, whereas the Israelis prepared their plan thoroughly before the two excursions – the SAS plan would suffer accordingly.

The defences around Stanley were not as formidable as those on Green Island, but there were 8000 Argentinian soldiers in and around the town, plus 105mm and 155mm artillery, anti-aircraft guns and Panhard armoured cars – enough firepower to blow the raiders out of the water. The SAS – two troops from D Squadron, one from G Squadron and six SBS men – approached the target in Rigid Raiders. They were supported by additional SAS soldiers, who descended from Murrell Heights on the northern shore of the harbour approach and put down a barrage of GPMG fire and Milan missiles. There was also naval gunfire support from the frigate *Arrow*.

In 1969 the Israelis had approached Green Island and then swum underwater for 15 minutes on the final leg of the journey, but the SAS had gone all the way to the target in their boats. Once on the island, Almog and his men could not initially find a way through the defences – a potentially disastrous situation. However, he then spotted a gap and signalled to his men. The shooting of two guards with Uzis signalled the Israelis' presence and the start of the assault.

One of the worst things that can happen to an assault team is to be discovered on the surface of the water, and this is what happened to the SAS force as it made its way towards its target. Searchlights from the hospital ship *Bahia Paraiso*, which was moored in the harbour, spotted the Rigid Raiders. The small craft then came under a hail of fire from Wireless Ridge and Stanley, with Argentinian 20mm anti-aircraft guns pouring streams of tracer in the direction of the little boats. The assault force, faced with certain annihilation, did the only sensible thing and beat a speedy retreat. The SAS reached the safety of the shore after suffering three minor casualties, and four badly holed boats. The SAS soldiers were particularly aggrieved by the actions of the hospital ship, which had used its lights to highlight the boats, the SAS had, according to the rules of war, not shot at it. Ironically, it was hit by Argentinian gunfire during the action.

The subsequent explosion destroyed the radar station and the fort

The Israeli commandos fared better on the night of 19/20 July 1969. They went on to deal with the Egyptian defenders with a mixture of grenades and small-arms fire and placed their demolition charges. They were then evacuated by the inflatables before the charges went off and the Egyptians on the mainland were alerted. The subsequent explosion destroyed the radar station and wrecked the fort. This daring action cost the Israelis six killed and 10 wounded.

Though elite units such as the SAS continue to train for maritime operations, special forces in general are facing a dilemma about waterborne missions. As the twenty-first century approaches, maritime insertion techniques are becoming increasingly complicated and risky, and this is as true for the SAS as it is for other elite units.

Above: Israeli Naval Commandos such as these conducted the daring assault on Green Island. Note their Soviet weapons.

Many Third World nations, for example, are spending a lot of money on military equipment and the defence of their land and territorial waters. Their elite forces are trained by Western firms employing ex-special forces personnel, including former Special Air Service soldiers. This means that waters are becoming increasingly dangerous for military swimmer-canoeists.

So who is the best? In terms of training and equipment, the COMSUBIN must be considered the best all-round elite maritime unit, because the SAS devotes only part of its resources to its maritime role. However, the Regiment is certainly as good as the world's larger maritime formations, such as the US Marine Corps and Royal Marines, in terms of tactical flexibility, and can hold its own against the SEALs and SBS.

BY AIR

In terms of military units 'airborne' is synonymous with 'elite'. But what is the actual airborne role of the world's premier elite unit – the Special Air Service – what aircraft does it use, and how good is it in this area compared with other units?

This chapter looks at the SAS's airborne role, training, equipment and actions and compares them with those of the other top-flight special forces airborne units and formations – the French Foreign Legion's 2nd REP, Spetsnaz, the Australian SAS, the US 101st Airborne Division, the US 82nd Airborne Division, the British Parachute Regiment, Delta Force and the Israeli Parachute Corps – to determine which is the best airborne outfit.

The airborne role of the SAS is to insert teams into and extract teams from enemy territory when the occasion demands it. All troopers are parachute trained, but each Sabre Squadron has an Air Troop that specialises in freefall parachuting. Since men are rotated through the various troops during their SAS service, they will eventually gain experience of freefall parachuting and of working with helicopters. How does this compare with other units?

The French Foreign Legion's 2nd REP is a dedicated parachute unit that can deliver its men into enemy territory, though once they have landed the Legionnaires fight as conventional light infantry.

British special forces parachutists photographed prior to making a HALO jump from a Hercules transport aircraft. Note the altimeters and oxygen breathing equipment.

Russia's Spetsnaz has no airborne role as such. Parachuting is just one, increasingly unimportant, form of insertion for Russia's elite soldiers. Though they may be used as the spearhead of an airborne assault, there may be other, better, means of insertion for pathfinder and diversionary teams – in Afghanistan, for example, Spetsnaz teams arrived by helicopter. Most Soviet battle plans involved teams being inserted into their operational areas by commercial flights during the transition to war. During the Warsaw Pact invasion of Czechoslovakia in August 1968, for example, Spetsnaz personnel arrived at Prague's Ruzyne Airport in civilian Aeroflot aircraft. Alternatively teams were to make land infiltrations on foot into forward NATO areas by literally walking across the West's open borders.

The SAS has taken over the training and running of surveillance units

In airborne terms, the Australian SAS is markedly different from its British counterpart: it has no airborne role as such (that is covered by the Royal Australian Regiment), though its members do receive comprehensive parachute training. Because of Australian topography, Australian SAS airborne insertions have a number of peculiarities. For example, the unit prefers water jumps. Insertions into operational areas near coastlines or waterways may involve a static-line jump with canoes or inflatables, while inland Land Rovers will be dropped with the troops (one thing is certain: you don't drop a patrol into the Australian outback without some sort of vehicle backup). Within each squadron there is a Freefall Troop that is trained in HALO and HAHO techniques.

Nevertheless, for the Australians, the practicalities of wartime operations militates against parachute drops. For one thing, large supply drops, which are essential to Australian special forces if they are to operate successfully in remote regions, absorb too many transport aircraft. What is more, in wartime, parachute insertion may be unnecessary, as the SAS has taken over the training and running of north coast surveillance units like NORFORCE,

which, with their buried caches of supplies and equipment, provide an in situ guerrilla force.

One of the most famous airborne units in the world is Britain's Parachute Regiment. Currently, two of the regiment's three battalions are grouped within 5 Airborne Brigade, a formation designed to undertake a variety of missions, including 'Out of Area' operations. The primary

role of the Paras is to be a force capable of mounting fast, parachute insertion without support by employing static-line drops. But this appears increasingly unlikely (see below). Meanwhile the Americans possess two formations that have a dedicated airborne role. The 101st Airborne Division is tasked with 'Out of Area' operations, while the 82nd Airborne

Above: Soldiers of Britain's Parachute Regiment prepare to make a static-line jump. Many SAS soldiers come from the Paras.

Division is on standby as a 'no notice' rapid reaction force.

These, then, are the airborne roles of the SAS and its counterparts, but how do the

Above: The CH-47 Chinook helicopter. This particular model was used by the SAS in the Gulf War to deliver teams behind enemy lines.

airborne training courses measure up when compared to each other?

Prospective SAS recruits are introduced to parachuting at a relatively early stage of their training. The last phase of Continuation Training is a four-week static-line parachute course held at RAF Brize Norton in Oxfordshire (see Selection and Training Chapter). However, this type of parachuting – where the soldiers exit the aircraft and the parachute is opened at a predetermined height by a line connected to the aircraft – is rarely used by today's SAS soldiers. Instead, they use High Altitude, Low Opening (HALO) or High Altitude, High Opening (HAHO) techniques, and training in these methods is conducted after Continuation.

A HALO descent requires an exit from an aircraft at an altitude of 10,000m and a freefall descent to an altitude of 760m, when the 'chute will deploy automatically. The major advantage with HALO descents is that a team can land together (there is little drift when the team is in the air), which means no time is wasted rounding up individuals at the drop zone.

Such techniques require intensive training. SAS soldiers therefore attend a six-week HALO course at Brize Norton, which involves each student making around 40 descents. Recruits are taught how to jump by day and night while carrying up to 50kg of equipment and how to cope with the problems that are associated with HALO parachuting: ice on goggles, the danger of mid-air collision, the difficulty of manoeuvring in the air and so on. Members of SAS Boat Troops are also trained to make freefall jumps into the sea.

Despite the training undertaken by SAS soldiers, HALO insertion is rarely, if ever, used on operations. Significantly, it was turned down by SAS commanders in the Falklands and Gulf on the grounds of excessive risk. Nevertheless, HALO parachuting is an option the Regiment wants to retain for its missions, and SAS instructors also consider it to be a 'good character builder' for individuals.

HAHO parachuting is regarded as a way of increasing the Regiment's capacity for airborne insertion. With this technique a trooper exits the aircraft at an altitude of 10,000m, freefalls for 8-10 seconds and then opens his 'chute. He then makes a gentle descent to the ground – this can take up to 80 minutes – by which time he will have travelled up to 40km. Because SAS parachutists can stay in the air for so long, they can be dropped a long way away from the eventual target. This means the aircraft can remain outside the range of enemy radars, thus reducing the chances of the operation being compromised. How does this compare to the training provided in other units?

Each Australian SAS squadron has a Freefall Troop

The SAS appears to be a long way ahead of other formations. For example, even in dedicated parachute units like the French Foreign Legion's 2nd REP, the only members trained in HALO and HAHO operations are the Reconnaissance and Deep Action Commandos platoon (*Commandos de Renseignement et de l'Action en Profondeur* – CRAPS). All the others are trained in static-line jumps, but actual air operations within the regiment are the speciality of No 1 Company, which is trained in heliborne operations. And whereas all members of the 2nd REP do enough jumps each year to remain parachute qualified, only CRAPS and No 1 Company are heavily involved in training for airborne insertion.

As mentioned above, each Australian SAS squadron has a Freefall Troop which is trained in HALO and HAHO parachuting techniques. However, outside this troop parachute training is limited to only four or five static-line jumps each year. This is undertaken at the Parachute Training School at HMAS *Albatross*, near Nowra in New South Wales.

The amount of time devoted to training in the US 82nd and 101st Airborne Divisions is large because air mobility is their primary asset. Thus, each year the 82nd Airborne undergoes training in the Mojave Desert, the Alaskan wilderness or the Panamanian jungle, with all exercises involving parachuting and air landing. The division also takes part in annual 'no notice' exercises overseas, which also stress air mobility. The 101st undergoes a similar round of annual training, and even within the technical and support elements of both divisions a large part of exercises revolves around getting the men and equipment to the operational area.

There is little or no tactical parachuting within the 101st Airborne

In the 101st Airborne, the vast majority of the 800 members of each of the nine air assault battalions are parachute-trained, as are many of the support troops and helicopter pilots. However, there is little or no tactical parachuting within the 101st Airborne beyond maintaining the basic qualification – men and equipment are inserted by helicopter. In the 82nd Airborne Division, all infantry and support personnel pass through the 4th Airborne Training Battalion and the Basic Airborne Course at Fort Benning. In the main, though, parachuting is restricted to static-line drops.

In the British Parachute Regiment, less and less time is being spent on parachute training, and the regiment has often been forced to resort to balloon jumps to maintain the required number of annual jumps. The only unit that devotes a lot of time to parachute training is Pathfinder Platoon, which specialises in HALO/HAHO techniques (see Selection and Training Chapter). The last time The Parachute Regiment conducted a wartime drop was at Suez in 1956!

That is not to say that parachute drops onto a 'hot' landing zone are a thing of the past. For example, during Operation 'Just Cause', the US invasion of Panama in December 1989, units of the 82nd Airborne Division captured Torrijos Airport after dropping onto it. Similarly, during the US invasion of Grenada in October 1983, US Army Rangers made a parachute drop into Point Salines to secure the runway and clear obstacles to allow aircraft to land. In addition, elite units have made jumps as part of a hostage-rescue operations. For example, in May 1978 the French Foreign Legion's 2nd REP conducted a jump into Kolwezi, Zaire, to rescue 3000 Westerners from 4000 Katangan rebels. The operation was a success, though some of the Legionnaires were widely scattered after landing.

It can be said, therefore, that the SAS is probably the best parachute-trained unit in the world in terms of time devoted to parachuting and different types of parachute techniques – ahead, even, of dedicated airborne units such as the British Parachute Regiment and the US 82nd Airborne Division.

Airborne training is important, but airborne units also require aircraft – fixed-wing and rotary-wing – and also parachutes to carry out their missions. We will look at each in turn, and compare the SAS's with those in service with other units to determine who has the best. First, let us consider rotary-wing aircraft.

Just as the helicopter has had a profound effect on the battlefield by increasing mobility and anti-armour capabilities, it has also made an impact upon special forces operations since the late 1950s. During World War II, when helicopters had not yet made their debut on the battlefield, SAS teams were inserted into operational areas by parachute. They were dropped along with their equipment, such as jeeps, which were packed into crates and could make a large hole in the ground if the 'chutes didn't work properly. During the 1991 Gulf War against Iraq – which witness the largest concentration of British SAS troops on the ground since World War II – there were no SAS parachute insertions, but there were many SAS heliborne missions.

Below: A Sea King helicopter, as used by the SAS in the Falklands, swoops in to pick up a waiting special forces team in the Arctic.

Above: The Hind attack helicopter was used in Afghanistan to support Spetsnaz operations. Hinds usually worked in pairs to deliver fire support.

In many ways the helicopter is ideally suited to special forces operations, because it is able to land and take off vertically, hover, fly at low speeds and make severe turns. This means it can fly nap-of-the-earth, and make maximum use of terrain cover and take advantage of the poor performance of radar at very low altitude. Often radar cannot detect targets below the horizon and so aircraft can avoid detection by flying low enough to be shielded by the folds in the terrain – though this requires great skill from the pilots. Helicopters do have disadvantages, however: they are noisy (though the sound of engines and rotors can be reduced to a low level), vulnerable to ground fire and have relatively low top speeds due to the limitations of rotor aerodynamics.

The advantages of the helicopter as a vehicle for insertion were quickly spotted by the SAS. The Regiment first used them during the campaign in Malaya (1948-60), when Whirlwind and Dragonfly models were used to deliver supplies, evacuate casualties and transport troops. Today, the Regiment makes use of a number of helicopters, with aircraft supplied by the Army Air Corps 'S' Flight and the RAF's Special Forces Flight, part of No 7 Squadron, based at Odiham. Types available include the CH-47 Chinook, which was used to transport the SAS road watch patrols to their destination during the 1991 Gulf War; the Westland Sea King, which was used by the Regiment in the Falklands; and the AH-7 Lynx and Gazelle, both of which are used in Northern Ireland.

The SAS uses helicopters primarily for insertion and extraction. Other units make use of them for a variety of tasks. The US 82nd Airborne Division's Combat Aviation Battalion (CAB), for example, is primarily responsible for

aerial anti-tank missions and providing transport for heliborne assaults. It has 98 helicopters, including Sikorsky UH-60 Black Hawks, Bell AH-1S Cobras in the anti-armour role and OH-58 Kiowas in the reconnaissance role. The division's 1st Squadron, 17th Air Cavalry, is responsible for tactical reconnaissance, for calling in artillery fire and air support, and for engaging targets with its Cobra-mounted TOW missiles. Forward reconnaissance is conducted by the helicopter-mounted Aero-rifle Platoon.

The 101st Airborne Division is the US Army's only air assault division and contains 15,000 personnel, 54 howitzers and 373 helicopters, including Black Hawks, Cobras, Kiowas and Chinooks. Helicopters are the means by which the division fights – i.e. the scout aircraft precede the air-mobile infantry and artillery, which are in turn supported by the Cobra attack helicopters.

Above: 'Tree-jumping', a method of insertion invented by the SAS during the Malayan conflict. It was abandoned following a number of fatalities.

Another American unit that makes use of helicopters is Delta Force, though it doesn't have an airborne role as such. Aircraft are just a means of conducting missions and delivering teams to the target. Delta is assigned a range of helicopter assets, such as Sikorsky RH-53E Super Stallion transports. All Delta dedicated helicopters are provided by US Special Operations Command's (USSOCOM's) Special Operations Brigade based at Hunter Army Airfield, Georgia. The 160th Aviation Battalion is part of the Brigade and comprises 80 helicopters and 1000 personnel, including AH-6s, OH-58Ds equipped with Hellfire anti-tank missiles and MH-47s, the special operations version of the Chinook.

Spetsnaz units do not have dedicated air assets as such, though they do have access to the army's helicopters. In Afghanistan, for example, Spetsnaz units made wide use of helicopters, especially Hind assault and Hip transport models. Both types were used to insert troops on hill crests as part of general convoy escort duties or to attack Mujahedeen bases, operating either independently or in conjunction with Soviet mechanised units. The lessons learned in Afghanistan – where helicopters saved Spetsnaz foot patrols long forced marches in pursuit of Mujahedeen units – made helicopter insertion an important part of the Spetsnaz art of war.

Britain's Parachute Regiment has no tactical role using helicopters

Traditionally, the Australian SAS had the services of No 9 Squadron, Royal Australian Air Force, during their early years in Borneo and Vietnam. In Vietnam, the support helicopters were UH-1B gunships and UH-1D Huey transports. The unit still uses Hueys, along with the newer Black Hawks. The Australians have never embraced helicopters to the same extent as the Americans or the British, and in Vietnam their Air Wing was ambivalent about rotary-wing aircraft. The criticisms that were raised are still relevant: helicopters are noisy, they attract the enemy and they can only carry foot patrols. In addition, once again the Australians have geographical considerations to bear in mind when they select their aircraft (see above): the vast distances involved mean that helicopters require tanker support. If a tanker aircraft is going to be despatched, teams might as well be sent out by aircraft in the first place.

Britain's Parachute Regiment has no tactical role using helicopters, though they are used to transport Para companies on some exercises, as well as for inserting and extracting reconnaissance platoons in Northern Ireland. However, the creation of NATO's Rapid Reaction Force, of which 5 Airborne Brigade is an integral part, may see the Paras assuming a greater heliborne role. The regiment has two battalions grouped within 5 Airborne Brigade, which deploys its own Lynx and Gazelle helicopters for reconnaissance, casualty evacuation and the transport of ammunition and support weapons.

Israeli paratroopers devote a lot of time to helicopter training. In addition to their reconnaissance, special assault and counter-terrorist responsibilities, they are the spearhead of the Israeli Army's anti-tank force. They use Israeli-modified Sikorsky CH-53s as troop carriers, Bell 212s for aero-medical evacuation and Israeli Air Force AH-64A Apaches, Bell AH-1S Cobras and Hughes 500 MD Defenders in the support role. These last types were used to attack bridges and artillery positions in Lebanon during the 1982 Israeli invasion.

What can be said about these different helicopters in terms of performance and suitability for special forces missions? The SAS uses the Chinook, for example, so do the Americans for their elite missions. It is an excellent aircraft. The Sea King is a very reliable aircraft, whereas the Black Hawk and Stallions have had reliability problems on operations. Russian helicopters tend to be very basic and unsophisticated compared with Western models, though they are robust. Overall, in the Sea King and Chinook, the SAS has two of the best helicopters currently available.

The SAS has the use of aircraft provided by 47 Squadron.

Though parachuting is possible from helicopters, fixed-wing aircraft have traditionally provided the platform from which special forces teams have made their jumps. When the SAS began in World War II they used old bombers. Now the Regiment has the use of aircraft provided by RAF Special Forces Flight, 47 Squadron, based at RAF Lyneham. These are C-130 Hercules long-range transports, which are also used to support Parachute Regiment deployments.

The British Special Air Service also relies on fixed-wing aircraft for non-parachute duties: supply, deployment to areas prior to missions and evacuation. In the Hercules the Regiment has an aircraft that is ideally suited to support special operations. It can take off and land from rough airstrips, it is fitted with a probe for aerial refuelling, giving it an unlimited range; it has a large payload capacity, and it has an all-weather operational capability. In addition, and most importantly for elite units, it is very rugged.

Russia's Spetsnaz has an impressive range of aircraft to support missions, both for supply purposes and to conduct parachute drops. There are over 350 Russian military transport aircraft

on call, including An-12 Cubs, An-22 Cocks, An-124 Condors and Il-76 Candids. In addition, there is the new An-70 transport aircraft, which is the replacement for the Cub. All these aircraft

Below: Traditional static-line 'chutes have poor steerability and are generally employed by conventional airborne formations.

are reliable, though they are technologically behind their Western counterparts.

One of the most interesting aircraft to be used by Spetsnaz, however, is the An-2, a biplane that is fabric-covered and flies at a speed of 90km/hr. These qualities make it invisible to Doppler (where the motion of the target causes light, sound or radio waves) and Pulse (where return echoes are used to determine target range) radar. This means a Spetsnaz 14-man team, flying at tree-top level, can arrive at its target undetected – a scenario that worried NATO planners during the Cold War.

The AC-130 Spectre has a side-firing weapon system

Typically, the Americans have a wide variety of aircraft optimised for special forces operations. Delta Force, for example, can call upon the services of a clandestine Central Intelligence Agency (CIA)/Army aviation unit called 'Seaspray'. This is used both for Delta operations and deniable CIA missions, and consists mainly of light aircraft that are difficult to spot on radar and can use rough airstrips. The Twin Otter was used to lay the beacons and conduct the pathfinding survey at Desert One, the site in southern Iran chosen as the first stage of the abortive Delta Force attempt to rescue American hostages in Iran in April 1980.

The US Air Force's 23rd Air Force and 2nd Air Division supplies the 1st Special Operations Wing, which is tasked by the Office of Air Force Special Operations with providing US Air Force unconventional warfare capability. There are currently 13 Special Operations Squadrons equipped with MC-130E Combat Talon, MC-130H Talon II and AC-130H Spectre aircraft, as well as specialist helicopters.

The Combat Talon is a special operations variant of the C-130 Hercules. It is equipped with terrain-following radar, precision navigation and air-drop equipment, aerial refuelling probe, electronic countermeasures and the Fulton Surface-to-Air Recovery (STAR) system. The latter is a safe and rapid method of picking up a person from either land or water. A helium-filled balloon attached to a nylon cord is sent into the

Above: The mattress-type parachute is a more controllable, accurate and reliable insertion tool for elite teams than the static-line 'chute.

air by the person awaiting recovery. The aircraft swoops in and intercepts the line by means of the Y-shaped fork attached to the nose. The person, fitted with a harness that is attached to the line, is then lifted off the ground and pulled behind the aircraft. The aircrew, using a winch, then reels him or her aboard.

The AC-130 Spectre gunship is a modified Hercules with a side-firing weapon system. Equipped with aerial refuelling probes, the Spectre's mission brief includes close air support, interdiction, armed reconnaissance and air defence. Spectres proved particularly effective during the US invasion of Grenada when they provided support for the Rangers who parachuted onto the airfield at Point Salines on the first day of the invasion – 25 October

1983. Three gunships were used to clear anti-aircraft guns from around the airfield. Armed with 20mm, 40mm and 105mm cannon, the Spectres silenced the 23mm Soviet-built anti-aircraft guns defending the Point Salines within 45 minutes, though not before a number of hits had been scored on the gunships themselves. As one Spectre crew member remarked: 'The 2500 rounds per minute really cleared the crews from the anti-aircraft guns.'

As with helicopters, there is, in truth, very little to choose between the fixed-wing aircraft currently in use with elite units, though in the C-130 Hercules the SAS has one of the most durable transport aircraft in the world. With regards to range, reliability, payload capacity and ability to use rough airstrips, few other aircraft can match it.

There is a danger of windchill as individuals plummet at 192km/hr

Let us now move on to the various parachutes in use. Though static-line parachuting still forms a part of SAS training (see Selection and Training Chapter), HALO and HAHO techniques are the principal means by which SAS soldiers conduct parachute missions. They require specialist equipment, such as oxygen breathing equipment, a helmet with headset and an altimeter. However, the most important piece of kit is the parachute itself. A standard parachute has a low glide ratio, and so one opened at HAHO altitudes would keep its wearer in the air for only 10 minutes, and would land only 5km from the release point. In contrast, the steerable wing and foil canopies used by units such as the SAS, like the GQ 360 nine-cell flat ramair canopy model, have the same aerodynamic properties as an aircraft wing. Their low rate of descent and high forward speed allow the parachutist to travel up to 40km over a period of up to 80 minutes.

HAHO teams can leave the aircraft outside enemy territory and then drift towards the DZ. Usually conducted at night, HAHO operations carry a number of risks. First, the team must try to stick together in order to land in a tight formation. To this end, some parachutes have panels coated with a luminous material that

emits a dull glow and allows the men to remain in visual contact and avoid mid-air collisions. Second, there is the danger of the team drifting off course. Chest-mounted navigation packs, based on the Global Positioning System (GPS), allow each parachutist to check his position and amend his flight path. Third, there is the danger of asphyxiation and frostbite (the temperature at 10,000m can be as low as minus 50 degrees F). Layers of warm clothing, gloves and balaclavas

Above: The C-130 Hercules long-range transport aircraft. SAS Hercules, which have refuelling probes, are based at RAF Lyneham.

prevent cold injuries, while oxygen bottles ensure the men can breathe.

HALO parachutists, on the other hand, need have only two or three minutes' supply of oxygen. However, they too face a number of dangers, such as stress-induced hyperventilation and barometric trauma (air in the intestine, ears and sinuses expands in response to the lower air pressure at high altitudes). In addition, there is also a danger of windchill as individuals plummet

at a rate of 192km/hr. Ice may form on goggles and altimeter. The freefaller can try to rub it off, but he has to ensure that while doing so his symmetry is preserved: SAS soldiers carry up to 55kg on a freefall and so their freedom to correct their posture is severely limited – if the load shifts they can go into an uncontrollable spin, with fatal results.

The Australian SAS, like its British counterpart, undertakes both static-line and HALO and HAHO training and employs both static-line and steerable 'chutes. The New Zealand SAS, too, includes both parachuting techniques in its training, though the likelihood of the Kiwis using parachute insertions for the defence of New Zealand seems extremely remote.

The standard static-line 'chute in US service is the T-10, though from 1986 the Americans started to phase in the steerable MC-1B used by the Rangers, which has a better safety record. Ironically, during the US invasion of Grenada in October 1983, the Rangers who dropped on Point Salines airfield used T-10 'chutes. They were dropped from minimum altitude carrying heavy loads. American HALO/HAHO 'chutes include the A/P28-3 and the MC-3.

Parachutes in service with Britain's Parachute Regiment are the static-line Irvin PX1 Mk 4 and the PR7 reserve. Israel's paratroopers originally used the EFA-672-12 main 'chute and T-10-R reserve for static-line jumps, but may have now changed to the US T-10. For high-altitude work the Israelis use foil and ramair parachutes similar to those of the Americans.

Below: The Russian An-2 Colt biplane, an aircraft that can deliver up to 14 Spetsnaz soldiers into enemy territory, and remain invisible to radar.

As with aircraft, the various parachutes used by elite teams are very much on a par with each other. The models used for HALO and HAHO drops are better than the static-line variety in terms of operational flexibility. Overall, the 'chutes produced by the British firm Irvin tend to be at the cutting edge of technology.

Whatever aircraft or parachutes are used by special forces teams, during operations they are at their most vulnerable on the way to the target and on the way back. Despite having sophisticated avionics that allow nap-of-the-earth flying, and boasting electronic countermeasures (electronic warfare equipment designed to degrade the performance of enemy radars, radio transmitters and weapon-guidance systems), aircraft

carrying elite units are essentially transports. They are thus slow when compared to fighters and attack aircraft. If they are discovered they can be shot down relatively easily, thus terminating the mission.

Helicopters are similarly vulnerable. The point was brought home during the assault by Delta Force on Richmond Hill prison during Operation 'Urgent Fury', the US invasion of Grenada. Comparing the assault with the SAS's use of helicopters at Pebble Island is an excellent way of illustrating how airborne insertions of elite units should be carried out, and what happens when they are not conducted properly.

The SAS was ordered to destroy the aircraft on the airstrip

The SAS raid on Pebble Island during the Falklands War was in response to the stationing of Argentinian aircraft there. The island itself is a desolate, windswept stretch of land some 35km long and is situated to the northwest of West Falkland. The Pucara, Turbo-Mentor and Skyvan aircraft stationed there would pose a grave threat to the British ground forces once they had landed on East Falkland. The SAS was therefore ordered to raid the airstrip and destroy the aircraft. Originally, the raiding party was tasked with not only destroying the aircraft, but also with eliminating their ground crews and the garrison on the island. However, due to strong headwinds the carrier HMS *Hermes*, from where the raid was launched, took longer to reach the flying-off point than expected – she had been well out to sea as a precaution against the threat of enemy airborne attack. This meant that the SAS party had only 30 minutes, not the 90 originally planned, to carry out the mission. The helicopters used to carry the men had to be back on *Hermes* before daylight, so that the carrier and her escorts were safe from enemy air attack.

The Delta Force assault on the Richmond Hill prison was in theory like the SAS action on Pebble Island, in that the plan was to transport the assault team to the target in helicopters for the men to then carry out a ground assault. However, the aim was not to destroy aircraft but to rescue prisoners from the prison and then evacuate them. The prison itself was surrounded by People's Revolutionary Army (PRA) installations. It was therefore heavily defended, and only the apparent threat of a massacre of the prisoners justified the mission. The transport to the prison was provided by Black Hawk helicopters of the 101st Airborne Division.

The plans for both Delta and the SAS required the teams to arrive at their destinations during darkness to maintain maximum secrecy. The Sea King helicopters of 846 Naval Air Squadron left *Hermes* very late on 14 May 1982. They were designed to fly in all weathers and were fitted with complete avionics suites. The Black Hawks transporting the Delta team were known as the 'Night Stalkers' because they specialised in night flying. 'Urgent Fury' was their first major operation, and the plan had been to assault Richmond Hill prison in darkness in the early hours of 25 October 1983. However, because it had taken longer than expected to prepare the nine helicopters – codenamed Task Force 160 – Delta was over five hours behind schedule when the aircraft approached the prison! A more cynical explanation of their late arrival is that different elements within the American task force were operating in different time zones, and that the orders were given out with just a time written on them, and no indication of whether it was Greenwich Mean Time or Eastern Standard Time that was meant. Whatever the truth, it resulted in the assault being made in daylight.

Pebble Island was a textbook example of how to carry out an elite mission

Three Sea Kings were used to transport the 45 men of D Squadron, 22 SAS, plus a Royal Naval gunfire support team, to Pebble Island. Members of the squadron's Boat Troop had already conducted a reconnaissance of the island, and the helicopters reached land without incident. Then the men debussed and marched to the target, achieving total surprise. The subsequent action was an illustration of what a small team can achieve when it has the element of surprise was maintained: six Pucaras, four Turbo-Mentors and a Skyvan aircraft were destroyed for the loss

of only one man wounded – it was a textbook example of how to conduct an elite mission.

What happened to the Delta Force team on Grenada, conversely, was an example of the dire consequences that can follow when a special forces operation goes wrong. The plan to attack the prison was ambitious from the start, but the loss of the cover of darkness, allied to the fact that the invasion had begun and therefore the Grenadans were on a state of high alert, particularly their anti-aircraft gunners, fatally compromised the mission.

The Delta team spent the rest of the day being pinned down

One Black Hawk was shot down crossing over the coast and, amazingly, a second peeled away from the assault group and circled overhead until help arrived, thus disobeying the cardinal rule that the mission takes precedence over the lives of those involved. The prison overlooks the town of St George's and is itself overlooked by Fort Frederick. Between the two settlements runs a valley, and into this valley flew the remaining seven helicopters. As soon as the aircraft entered the valley they came under fire.

There is some controversy about the number of helicopters lost in the assault. A Delta Force team member who took part in the raid insists that one was shot down and another lost after crashing, while another source maintains that a total of five were shot down. Whatever the truth, the plan to rescue the prisoners was impossible to implement, and the Delta team spent the rest of the day pinned down by enemy fire after leaving the aircraft. The mission was a complete failure, and it was the Delta Force team that had to be rescued. This mission is a terrible indictment of US special forces operational tactics.

The move away from large-scale military static-line drops means that the future of airborne operations rests with specialist units and heliborne forces. Even units such as the SAS have down-graded parachuting as a means of insertion, preferring helicopters or landborne techniques. This is in response to sophisticated enemy radar and anti-aircraft defences, allied to

the increased capabilities of rotary-wing aircraft and even fixed-wing aircraft.

Many units that are fully committed to the airborne role do not even have the required number of dedicated assets to fulfil their role – notable examples are 2nd REP and the Israeli Paras – and others do not have a clearly defined 'real world' role, most notably Britain's Parachute Regiment. In these formations parachute training is retained as a way of ensuring units are staffed by the 'right stuff' and to give formations tactical flexibility, but large-scale static-line jumps in wartime are a thing of the past. Notwithstanding the US invasion of Panama in 1989, where 5000 of the 26,000 troops committed made parachute jumps.

There may, however, be a window of opportunity as far as parachuting is concerned for units such as the SAS. Airborne insertion is still a key method by which elite teams can enter enemy territory. Indeed, it is becoming increasingly important, as waterborne insertion becomes more high-risk – see By Water

Above: The aftermath of Operation 'Prelim'. Wrecked Argentinian aircraft litter the airstrip on Pebble Island following the SAS raid.

Chapter. True, recent operations in the Gulf and the Falklands suggest that the helicopter is now the favoured means of delivery. However, as radar and detection methods become ever more sophisticated, clandestine heliborne insertion techniques may themselves become too high-risk for future operations, even with nap-of-the-earth flying, which runs the risk of the aircraft crashing into the terrain. If heliborne insertion does become too dangerous, elite forces may have to use HAHO parachuting as a means of inserting teams, either that or abandon airborne insertion altogether and rely on landborne infiltration into enemy territory, which means missions will take much longer.

But whether aircraft, helicopters or parachutes are used one thing is certain: the SAS will continue to be a world leader in carrying out airborne insertions.

COUNTER-TERRORISM

The SAS is but one of the 90 plus counter-terrorist units in the world. Which is the best when it comes to training, equipment, weapons and success against terrorists?

There are currently over 90 counter-terrorist/hostage-rescue (CT/HRU) units in the world. Many of these units have been established and trained by the SAS and other Western CT formations, and have thus adopted their equipment and tactics. This chapter will therefore concentrate on comparing the SAS with other Western units: GSG 9, GIGN, Delta Force, the FBI's Hostage Response Team, Comacchio Group, the Australian and New Zealand SAS and the Special Boat Service (SBS). Comparisons will be made concerning CT training, weapons, equipment and actual operations. The chapter will show that the British SAS has had a major influence on counter-terrorist tactics throughout the world, and has set the standards which other CT units aspire to. When it comes to hostage-rescue, few observers doubt that the SAS is the world's best.

The need for such units became urgent towards the end of the 1960s and early 1970s, when a plethora of international terrorist groups, headed by violent Palestinian factions, instigated a number of attacks against Western and Israeli targets which ranged from bombings to hostage taking and

A counter-terrorist soldier, equipped with respirator and armed with a Browning High Power handgun, photographed during a hostage-rescue drill. His suit is flame-proof.

assassinations. But the one incident, more than any other, that was to provide the catalyst for the formation of Western counter-terrorist units was the massacre of 11 Israeli athletes at the 1972 Munich Olympics.

On 5 September 1972, armed members of the Palestinian terrorist group Black September seized 11 Israeli sportsmen hostage at the Olympic village in Munich. Demanding the release of 234 prisoners held in Israel and members of the Red Army Faction incarcerated in West Germany, the terrorists and their hostages were eventually flown by helicopter to Furstenfeldbruk military airport. They had been informed that they would be flown to Cairo. However, as they left the helicopters hidden West German snipers opened fire, killing two terrorists and wounding others, as well as two helicopter crewmen. The other terrorists managed to get back to the helicopters, whereupon the West Germans mounted an assault with troops and armoured cars. The result was carnage, as the Palestinians killed five of the bound and gagged hostages in one helicopter and then blew it up, while the other helicopter exploded in the firefight. Though five terrorists had been killed and another three arrested, a total of 11 Israelis had been killed.

The Munich massacre sent shock waves throughout the West

The Munich massacre sent shock waves throughout western Europe and the United States, and individual governments took measures to make sure a repeat would not occur on their territory. Munich had demonstrated that local police forces, no matter how well trained, did not have the skills or expertise to deal with a determined terrorist attack. In Britain, Prime Minister Edward Heath ordered a specialist unit be created to deal with terrorist threats – one year after Munich the SAS's Counter Revolutionary Warfare (CRW) Wing was established at Hereford. In fact, the Regiment had already been thinking about counter-terrorism in the 1960s, and its commander at the time, Colonel John Waddy, had written a paper regarding the SAS's counter-terrorist role.

Hostage-rescue was, in many ways, a logical extension of the Regiment's CRW responsibility, which involves infiltrating enemy territory, intelligence gathering, ambushing and harassing insurgents, sabotage, border surveillance, implementing 'hearts and minds' policies, and training and liaising with friendly forces (the Australian SAS thought likewise, and assumed a CT role in 1979). In addition, many of the Regiment's soldiers were already trained as bodyguards, and had been sent on foreign assignments by the British government For example, following the end of the campaign in Aden in 1967, the SAS had offered the government its best marksmen for bodyguard duties, and the offer was readily accepted. The CRW Wing trains all Sabre Squadron personnel in counter-terrorism and hostage-rescue.

GSG 9 was to be drawn from the West German Border Police

Surprisingly, 22 SAS is not the only UK unit that has a counter-terrorist brief. For example, Comacchio Group was formed as a result of the British government's concern in the 1960s that 'subversives' might find employment in the oil industry. Comacchio Group is a 350-man security unit composed of hand-picked volunteers. Its tasks include: providing protection for Britain's Polaris and Trident nuclear submarines, both in harbour and during transit to the open seas; protecting the RAF's nuclear weapons; protecting all convoys carrying nuclear weapons; patrolling Loch Erne and other sea lochs in Northern Ireland to interdict IRA gun-running, and interdiction missions in commercial shipping lanes off Hong Kong to prevent drug smuggling, other contraband and piracy.

The SBS's CT role is involved with the protection of Britain's North Sea oilfields from terrorist attack and the safeguarding of UK shipping anywhere in the world. SBS CT exercises involve inflatables and helicopters and underwater approaches to targets with specialist equipment (see By Water Chapter). Britain therefore looked to its elite military units to provide a CT capacity, whereas the Germans looked to their police.

The men of Britain's 22nd Special Air Service Regiment sometimes refer to themselves as the 'pilgrims', a reference to a verse in the poem 'Hassan' by James Elroy Flecker that is inscribed on the Regimental clock at Hereford. It is a reference to their dedication to a spartan way of life. There is another unit that also adheres to this training philosophy, one which has come to rival the SAS in CT capability: Germany's *Grenzchutzgruppe 9* (GSG 9), or Border Marksmen Group 9.

Formed in the wake of the Munich massacre, the establishment of the unit was a major step for the West German government. Prior to the outrage, post-war West Germany had found it difficult to introduce effective counter-terrorist measures, which were often labelled 'fascist' by even moderate Germans. These problems were compounded by West Germany's attempts to forge relationships with Third World countries, especially in the Middle East. Consequently, the government was not prepared to authorise controversial 'high-profile' security arrangements at the Munich Olympics. However, in the aftermath of Munich new German laws were introduced, despite public opinion, which gave the police powers to detain terrorist suspects for longer periods and, when necessary, 'shoot to kill'. The government also decided to create a counter-terrorist unit. It was to be drawn from the West German Border Police, not the Army. There were two reasons for this. First, it was decided that a military elite with a 'political role' might be compared with Germany's wartime SS. Second, a federal police unit would have both powers of arrest and national authority.

France's CT unit, *Groupement d'Intervention de la Gendarmerie Nationale* (GIGN), like the SAS, was created from the military. France has always been the focus for terrorist activities. German occupation during World War II gave rise to communist and nationalist maquis resistance units determined to fight the Germans, as well as each other. This marked

Above: Two members of the FBI Hostage Response Team sharpen their shooting skills with Heckler & Koch MP5 submachine guns.

division between left and right was further aggravated in post-war France by the conflicts in Indo-China and Algeria. Between 1954 and 1962, while the conflict in Algeria raged, the fight between the *Algerian Front de la Libération Nationale* (FLN) and the right-wing *Organisation de l'Armée Secrète* (OAS) spilled onto the streets of France. Thus began a cycle of murder, bombings and assassination attempts. In the first week of May 1962, for example, there were over 200 murders. President de Gaulle responded to the terror by reorganising the intelligence service, which became the *Service de Documentation Extérieure et de Contre-Espionage* (SDECE). It was given wide-ranging powers and

urged to take the war to the enemy. This it did very effectively, with telephone tapping, gun-carrying secret service men and semi-official hired killers devising their own brand of 'counter-terror' to protect France and her interests at all costs.

The international terrorism of the 1970s, notably the Munich incident and the seizure of the Saudi Arabian Embassy in Paris in 1973, led to the French security services preparing to strike back. However, the numerous French counter-terrorist agencies were ineffective and began to squabble among themselves. As well as SDECE, a number of agencies responsible for counter-terrorism emerged and began to vie for supremacy: a greatly strengthened Security Service, *the Direction de la Surveillance du Territoire* (DST); the intelligence service of the police, *Renseignements Généraux*; the criminal police, *Police Judiciaire*; and the police anti-terrorist unit, *Service de Recherche d'Assistance d'Intervention et de Dissuasion*.

However, in November 1973 the French government decided to create a separate counter-terrorist unit out of the oldest serving regiment in the French Army: the *Gendarmerie Nationale*. It would handle politically sensitive hostage sieges, prison riots and the transport of dangerous prisoners. In addition, it was to be under direct political control and kept apart from the political in-fighting that embroiled the other agencies. The unit was named *Groupement d'Intervention de la Gendarmerie Nationale* (GIGN). The first commander was Lieutenant Prouteau, a black belt in Karate and a keen athlete, who quickly stamped his authority upon the men under his command.

The aim of the 'Killing House' is to polish individual and team skills

The Americans, too, looked to the military to provide a CT unit, forming Delta Force from their Special Forces. The unit is tasked with foreign counter-terrorist operations which involve the capture of hostaged US personnel, installations or property. It is also involved in the training of local security and intervention teams, as well as challenging and hardening the security of American overseas civilian facilities. Delta Force was established by Colonel Charles Beckwith, a US Special Forces veteran who served with the SAS in the early 1960s. As a result, Delta is closely modelled on the SAS.

For incidents inside the United States, the FBI's Hostage Response Team is used when criminals breach a federal law. As most incidents fall either to SWAT teams maintained by the state, city and county police or the Highway Patrol, or to federal intervention teams like the National Park Police, the number of incidents requiring the FBI intervention team is quite small. In view of this, the 50-man unit is part-time, only coming together for periodic training.

These, then, were the reasons Western CT units were created. But creating a unit is one thing: ensuring it can fulfil its requirement is another. Each formation had to devise CT

training structures to teach the unique skills needed to rescue hostages from armed terrorists. What does this training entail, and who has the best programme?

A major part of the training conducted by the SAS's CRW Wing involves acquiring proficiency in close quarter battle (CQB) techniques. This includes a six-week marksmanship course, but for training for specific hostage-rescue missions the SAS constructed the so-called 'Killing House' at Hereford. The sole aim of the building is to polish individual and team skills to a high level so that all members are thinking on the same wave length and aware of each other's actions. The House itself is full of corridors, small rooms and obstacles; the walls have a special rubber coating that absorbs the impact of rounds as they hit and prevents dangerous ricochets.

The rooms and corridors can be laid out by the instructors to simulate different types of buildings. The hostages will often be mixed in among the terrorists (dummies), who will be armed with a variety of weapons (knives, grenades and machine guns) to test individuals' reaction times (targets with guns are always engaged first as they pose the immediate threat).

At least one SAS soldier has been killed playing a hostage

To add realism to the exercises and to develop the team's confidence in using live ammunition, 'live' hostages are used, who sit at a table or stand on a marked spot, waiting to be 'rescued'. Though at least one SAS soldier has been killed while playing a hostage, the practice of using SAS soldiers as hostages continues. The CQB range also includes electronically operated figures that can be controlled by the instructors. In one scenario, for example, three figures, one of which is a terrorist, have their backs to team members as they enter a room. Suddenly, all three will turn and one will be armed. The SAS soldiers, in a split second, have to make a correct assessment and shoot the terrorist.

As the course continues the scenarios are made more difficult. The lights are normally switched off just prior to an assault (a basic standard operational procedure before a rescue team goes in). Smoke, gas and obstacles can be introduced to separate team members, with loud simulated shooting and screams and other disorientating noises.

All this training is designed to refine each man's speed, reactions and drills, until entry and clearance techniques become second nature. A large amount of resources are devoted to this aim. For example, in an average training week each man will fire around 5000 live rounds of ammunition in the 'Killing House'. Drills will be practised until every SAS trooper has become an effective part of a Sabre Squadron's Special Projects Team. There is always a squadron on 24-hour standby for intervention duties, and the squadron is split into four operational troops called Special Projects Teams. Each team is divided into four-man assault squads, which, during operations, are further divided into two-man teams (during assaults each man is assigned specific areas inside each room which are his responsibility to clear).

What does all this training achieve? It produces soldiers who can handle weapons with a dexterity that is quite amazing. For example, a fully trained SAS soldier can aim and fire the 13 rounds from a Browning High Power magazine in three seconds. As the critical period in clearing a room is the first four seconds, such accurate, heavy firepower is often the difference between success and failure and dead or live hostages (during every assault the aim is to kill all the terrorists).

Below: Somewhere in the English countryside, an SAS team fine-tunes its hostage-rescue skills. Success depends on speed and accurate shooting.

Above: Inside the 'Killing House' two soldiers engage targets. Note the two magazines taped together on the MP5 submachine gun.

The New Zealand SAS places its main emphasis on slick reaction and firing drills rather than sophisticated equipment for hostage-rescue operations, and employ the tried and tested MP5 submachine gun and Browning High Power handgun in training and on operations.

The Australian SAS allocates its No 1 Squadron of around 40 men to the counter-terrorist role. As in Britain, training is intensive, with practice assaults on vehicles, buildings (including high-rise structures), oil rigs and ships. There is a lot of emphasis on waterborne operations: since the SAS is more likely to be asked to intervene on an oil rig or gas platform than at a building in Sydney, divers and boats are free-dropped and parachute-inserted by Sea King helicopters of the Australian Navy. In fact, the squadron was once known as the 'Off-shore Assault Group', though it is now called the the Tactical Assault Group.

Away from the water, training concentrates on indoor and outdoor CQB ranges, a special 'urban complex' at Bindoon (which includes a plunging range for vertical firing) and aircraft mock-ups at Gin Gin airfield. Once a week troopers practice live firing interventions in a killing house. In addition, the SAS also has a 'Method of Entry House' at Bindoon.

One of the advantages of creating a counter-terrorist unit from an existing military elite is that individuals are already highly trained and highly fit soldiers, and are therefore adept at handling weapons and communications equipment. For units such as the GIGN and GSG 9, training courses had to be established to ensure each unit attracted the 'right stuff'. This means training courses are longer, though an advantage is that once trained a man tends to stay with the unit, and is not rotated through other non-CT troops or squadrons.

A major part of initial unit training is conducted outside GIGN

When an officer from France's Gendarmerie National applies to join GIGN, his record is scanned for disciplinary offences before he is granted an interview with the unit's commanding officer who decides whether each candidate has the qualities to enter the selection course.

To survive the first week of pre-selection, the candidate must successfully complete a 50m swim within 15 seconds, an 8km run, with equipment, in under 40 minutes and a 7m rope climb within seven seconds. His minimum shooting score must by 70 out of 100 at 25m for the handgun and 75 out of 100 with a rifle at 200m. Candidates also have to show the selectors that they have 'heart', which means facing tests of courage, such as fighting an unarmed combat instructor or an attack-trained dog. Only 1-10 per cent of the men go on from here to unit training. Thus GIGN has high standards, comparable with the SAS's.

A major part of initial unit training is conducted outside GIGN, with candidates who subsequently fail being returned to the Gendarmerie National. In this way GIGN does not have to waste precious time on unsuitable

Above: Two Uzi-armed GIGN divers come ashore. GIGN places great emphasis on underwater skills, and its arduous training reflects this.

candidates (initial training also acts as a selection course). The phases that are used for selection by GIGN are the standard diving and parachute courses.

After these courses comes physical training schedule to build fitness and stamina and then maintain it at a very high level. The punishing exercises include long cross-country runs interspersed with cycles of fast sprints. In addition, callisthenics and weight training prepare the men for the 'hard' Karate style taught in the unit (GIGN favours the full-contact style of Karate that is popular in France).

Diver training continues in the unit and the men progress to become combat swimmers, spending four hours a week underwater. Much of the training is conducted at night, as the optimum time for the insertion of swimmers during a hostage-rescue operation is under cover of darkness. Zero visibility places a new stress on the diver and can induce severe anxiety in a man who normally does not suffer from claustrophobia. To help prepare the men for night diving, the team sits on the muddy bottom of the River Seine, listening to the heavy barges pass overhead. When the divers feel comfortable, they switch off their torches and acclimatise to the dark, murky water. This training technique also gets individuals used to the sound of passing ships (the engine noise through the water makes the ships appear larger and closer than they actually are).

It may appear strange that a CT unit should devote so much time to combat swimming. Yet combat swimming is invaluable not only when mounting operations against a hijacked ocean liner, yacht or beach-side building, but also for other operations. For example, combat swimmers have been used during a train hijack! In May 1977, a Dutch train was seized by South Moluccan terrorists, who halted it at De Punt. Combat swimmers managed to swim up a canal that ran close to the tracks and attach heat detectors and sensitive listening devices to the outside of the train. These devices were used to keep track of the terrorists prior to the final assault. Thus a warm body (a person) that was carrying a long, cold object (a weapon) could be identified as one of the terrorists, even though he was out of sight of the snipers.

The GIGN man is expected to make the descent in under seven seconds

When the GIGN men are not in the water, much of their training is taken up with the core skills that are vital to the successful rescue of hostages: gaining entry to terrorist-held buildings and quickly immobilising or eliminating the terrorists. The unit puts great emphasis on abseiling techniques, as they are often the fastest way of gaining entry into a building. Teams may begin a descent from a roof if it is possible to climb up the side of the building unseen, or they may gain access from an adjoining building. Alternatively, the team can abseil out of a helicopter as it hovers above the building (this approach is noisy but fast, and the terrorists may be tricked into believing that the helicopter is coming in for a totally innocent reason). As a consequence, the unit carries out a lot of helicopter training, with teams practising abseiling onto a roof or using the pendulum technique that allows an operator to crash through a window. Abseiling from a hovering helicopter, the GIGN man is expected to make the descent in under seven seconds.

Comacchio Group, another unit that is heavily involved with waterborne operation, trains at the Special Boat Service (SBS) CQB/HRU school at Poole in Dorset. That part of the Company with a maritime brief is expected to recapture/help capture oil rigs, but can only intervene if requested to do so by the civil police. In contrast, military-grade nuclear

materials and weapons are always protected by an armed guard, and the men are expected to use lethal force to prevent capture of said materials (if the weapons are captured they become the responsibility of someone else).

In the past, Comacchio Group conducted intervention training scenarios on oil rigs as practice for hostage-rescue operations. However, maritime intervention missions now fall within the government's brief for the UK Special Force Group and are thus the responsibility of the SBS. This would seem to suggest that Comacchio Group now plays a subsidiary role.

There are two SBS killing houses, one to teach hostage-rescue drills and one for maritime counter-terrorism (MCT) techniques. The house that teaches MCT involves tactics and equipment pertinent to missions on the water. For example, a new fragmentation round has been specifically designed for storming ships and boats. When it hits a bulkhead it explodes on impact and does not ricochet, thus presenting no danger to the assault team.

Delta Force trains it men in the 'House of Horrors'

There are currently some 100 killing houses around the world, all designed to fine-tune the hostage-rescue skills of CT units. Though the most famous one is at Stirling Lines, the one possessed by Delta Force, called the 'House of Horrors', comes a close second. The house reportedly has four rooms: the first is a warm-up room containing pop-up friend-or-foe targets; the second has entry and immediate engagement scenarios; the third is set up for night shooting and assaults; and the fourth is a mock-up of an aircraft cabin.

As well as training in the house, Delta Force conducts covert air and underwater infiltration exercises (which are also carried out with SEAL Teams Five and Six), aircraft drills (in conjunction with the US Federal Aviation Authority), and assaults on buildings. A lot of time is spent on the range (15-20 hours a week), and other training includes use of explosives and breaching techniques, ordnance evaluation and disposal, first aid, high-speed and evasive driving, abseiling (helicopters and buildings) and new technology (particularly electronics and optics).

The training in other CT units is just as intensive. In GSG 9, for example, there is a strong emphasis on weapons training, and each officer will shoot over a million rounds a year to hone his reflexes with small arms. In GEO, each man will spend up to 12 hours a day practising shooting, demolitions, communications and combat swimming, in addition to night and weekend exercises.

The Italian CT unit *Nucleo Operativo Central di Sicurezza* (NOCS) places great emphasis on unarmed combat (Karate and Judo), abseiling, evasive and high-speed driving, demolitions, marksmanship, electronic surveillance, and terrorist psychology and organisation. With regard to tactics, NOCS prefers night assaults, and these feature strongly in training.

Marksmen in the pursuing helicopter will be in contact with the commander

Marksmanship plays an extremely important part in all CT units, and is regularly tested during exercises. In GSG 9, for example, during training scenarios each officer is scored on his marksmanship. Exercises involving GSG 9 Specialein-satztrupp (SET) combat teams incorporate their supporting Puma, Bell Huey and Bell 212 helicopters from the Special Air Transport Unit, and a fleet of highly tuned Volkswagen and Mercedes Benz vehicles (GSG 9 is composed of 120 officers divided into four strike units, with each strike unit being further divided into a command unit and five SETs). These exercises often involve the pursuit of 'terrorists' along the German autobahns. Scenarios are designed to test the whole unit, with the headquarters staff adjusting operational plans to allow for new developments, and the Communications Unit controlling and coordinating the SET pursuit teams, helicopters and supporting elements of the Traffic Police.

During these exercises, marksmen in the pursuing helicopter will be in constant radio contact with the Strike Unit commander and the overall controller in the Communications Unit.

When the decision to intervene has been made, marksmen stop the car by firing well-placed automatic bursts into the car's engine block. Simultaneously, other officers eliminate dummies representing key 'terrorists' (such as a person in the back seat holding a gun to the driver's head) with well-aimed single shots to the head. It is reported that these marksmen are able to score a hit more than 85 per cent of the time.

Counter-terrorist work requires a wide range of weapons and equipment

CT sniping requires marksmen remaining in position for long periods, sometimes for hours at a time, until the assault goes in. Traditionally the CT sniper is part of a well-coordinated plan, whose main role is to cover the assault. However, this is not the case in some CT units. In India, for example, the National Security Guard, which is composed of the 4000-strong Special Action Group and the 2300-strong Special Ranger Group, splits its members into assault teams and snipers for interventions, but the snipers are trained to eliminate the greatest number of terrorists over several days before the assault takes place. The assaults themselves are just as crude, and resemble the D-Day commando attacks, i.e. create a breach in the defences and overwhelm the defenders by sheer force of number. While this may result in the deaths of probably all the terrorists, most of the hostages would also be killed. The Indians have much to learn about hostage-rescue!

In the final analysis there is very little to choose between the training courses of the various Western CT units, because they have shared ideas and all work towards the same aim: rapid, reliable and highly discriminative firepower to bring a hostage situation to a successful conclusion. In an aircraft, for example, the terrorists can be among the passengers. If CT team members are careless they risk shooting the hostages, but if they are too slow they risk the lives of the hostages. If one had to make a decision about which unit's training is the best, the only criterion for judging is actual operations – and in this regard, the SAS's record is second to none.

Above: If the door is blocked or guarded, abseil down the side of the building and enter uninvited via the windows. Don't forget to do it in style.

Counter-terrorist work requires a wide range of specialist weapons and equipment. What does the SAS use, and how does it compare to the kit of other units? Advanced technology is a double-edged sword when it comes to hostage-rescue. On the one hand, advances in body armour and ammunition mean that assault team members are better protected and armed then previously. Nevertheless, there is the ever-present danger of malfunction when using advanced technology, with often disastrous consequences. For example, during Delta Force's attempt to free the American hostages held in Iran in April 1980, three of the RH-53D Sea Stallion helicopters that were crucial to the mission had to abort due to technical problems and the mission was fatally compromised. The British SAS has an Operations Research Wing at Hereford that tests, evaluates and designs equipment for use by the Regiment in hostage-rescue operations.

Assault team members storming buildings must be protected against heat, fire, smoke and blast (the Iranian Embassy caught fire during the SAS rescue in May 1980), and must wear body armour as protection against bullets. All SAS assault team members use the GD Specialist Supplies suit made from Nomex. The suit incorporates a respirator hood and flame barrier felt pads in the knees and elbows. Fireproof gloves are also worn.

There is a wide range of body armour available, and the SAS currently uses Armourshield's GPV (General Purpose Vest) 25, which gives wrap-around protection. In addition, ceramic plates can be worn over the vest, giving the wearer protection against high-velocity and armour-piercing rounds. However, there is a weight penalty with body armour. For example, the ceramic plates alone can weigh up to 4kg each. Despite this, all hostage-rescue units employ some sort of ballistic armour.

Headgear is a very important part of an assault team member's equipment, and so the SAS is equipped with the AC/100/1 helmet. Designed to be worn over a headset and

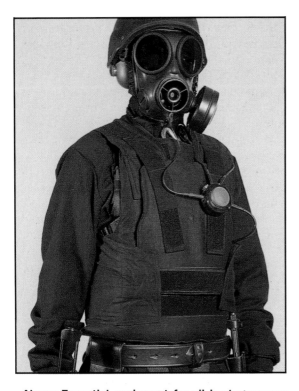

Above: Essential equipment for all hostage-rescue operatives: helmet, respirator, body armour and communications set.

respirator, it is made from multiple layers of ballistic-resistant composite materials. During an assault it is imperative that the heads of team members are protected from bullets and falling debris, and so helmets have integral high impact trauma liners to dissipate the energy of any blow they may suffer. As with body armour, all hostage-rescue units use some sort of head protection.

Prior to an assault, tear gas and coloured smoke may be fired into a building to disorientate the terrorists, explosives may be used to force an entry, stun grenades may be thrown in to disorientate hostiles, and shotguns may be used to blow open doors. Such actions may result in materials, such as curtains, seats and carpets, catching fire, producing thick, toxic smoke. If the terrorists' eyes are blinded by smoke and they cannot breathe easily, the assault team obviously has an advantage – provided they themselves can see and breathe. Therefore, respirators are an essential item for the CT

Communications are extremely important during an assault, both between team members and the team leader and support and command elements. With the SF10 communications are possible by direct speech at short range and by radio, via a microphone mounted in front of the lips which is linked to a radio transmitter.

There are other items of equipment that are integral to hostage-rescue missions. Abseiling kit, for example, is essential for rapid descent of team members down the side of a building. There are usually three items of equipment: rope, harness and descendeur (a metal device, clipped to the harness, through which the rope is threaded), which allow a trooper to control his rate of descent.

Infra-red night scopes can be used to identify terrorists on the darkest night

Photographs of the SAS at the Iranian Embassy in 1980 showed black-clad soldiers storming the building. Other hostage-rescue units also equip their members with black assault suits. This may seem irrelevant to the success or failure of a mission. However, there is a very good reason for the suits: the sinister black uniform gives the team a psychological edge.

Because the timing of an assault is so essential to the success of a hostage-rescue operation, the unit must collect as much intelligence beforehand concerning the where-abouts of the terrorists and their hostages. Therefore, CT operatives must be able to use intelligence-gathering and surveillance technology. This equipment includes thermal imaging systems that can detect human beings because their body temperature is much higher than that of their surroundings. Weapons are much colder, and thus the device can tell you if the suspects are armed and even their location in the building. Using the same principle, infra-red night scopes can be used to identify terrorists on the darkest night or through dense smoke.

Parabolic microphones use a dish to collect the sound waves from a conversation several hundred metres away. Other devices can pick up the voices of terrorists speaking inside a room in a distant building. They deflect a laser off window panes and pick up small vibrations in the glass caused by the sound waves in the room. The returning signal is electronically decoded back into speech. Another useful instrument is the fibre optic light scope, which is as thin as a piece of wire but, once inserted into the wall of a room, the small fish-eye lens at the end produces a panoramic view of everything that is going on inside the room.

Submachine guns combine maximum firepower with minimum weight

What about other CT units? Though they may use different suppliers to the SAS, nearly all formations kit out their assault teams in similar equipment: helmets, body armour and respirators. The equipment used by NOCS, GIGN, GSG 9 and the Americans is just as good as that employed by the SAS. What about weapons?

Once an assault has been decided upon, the team will have to use lethal force to bring the siege to a successful close (it is only in Hollywood films that officers shoot to wound). The choice of weapons for hostage-rescue work is therefore critical. Assault teams must have weapons that are compact, reliable, accurate, and that have a full-automatic capacity and good balance. The submachine gun combines maximum firepower with minimum weight, and is therefore the primary weapon for CT assault teams. One model in particular is in widespread use, mainly because it is used by the SAS: the Heckler & Koch MP5.

Why is the MP5 so popular among CT units? There are two main reasons. First, it fires from a closed bolt. Most submachine guns fire from an open bolt, which means the bolt flies forward to chamber a round when the trigger is pulled. This produces a shift in the gun's balance, which usually results in the shot being off target. With the MP5, however, the bolt is closed when the trigger is pulled (the only thing that moves is the hammer, which fires the cartridge), and so there is no shift in balance. Second, and just as important, the MP5 is a very reliable weapon. The MP5 is currently in widespread use with CT units, such as GIGN,

GSG 9, Delta Force, Spain's *Grupo Especial de Operaciones* (GEO), the FBI's Hostage Response Team and the Australian SAS, plus a host of Third World CT units.

Another weapon that has found favour with CT units is the Browning High Power, a semi-automatic handgun that is used by the British and Australian SAS. Traditionally backup weapons, handguns can also be used in the primary role, such as when a point man wants to carry a stun grenade, or for confined spaces where it is difficult to wield a submachine gun.

As CT units are traditionally allocated generous budgets, money is no problem when it comes to purchasing sophisticated weaponry. As a result, they often possess some superb equipment. For example, GSG 9 employs the highly accurate Heckler & Koch PSG1 sniper rifle, complete with night scopes, and the superbly made Mauser M66 sniper rifle.

One of the most effective weapons is the stun grenade

One of the most effective weapons in the CT soldier's armoury is the stun grenade. Originally designed by the SAS, it has been successfully used by the Regiment and other hostage-rescue units. Essentially a diversionary device that produces a blinding flash and loud bang (hence its nickname 'flash bang'), it disorientates a terrorist long enough for an assault team member to kill him or her.

As with assault clothing and equipment, most of the CT weapons used are indigenous to all units, specifically the MP5 and High Power. It is thus difficult to make comparisons. The cooperation and sharing of intelligence between CT units has resulted in this duplication of hardware use. It has also had other advantages.

Just as international terrorism has spread across borders and continents, those responsible for defeating the agents of terror have banded together to fight the common foe. From the very beginning there has been a high level of co-operation and cross-training between CT units, and in the forefront of this has been the SAS. For example, the SAS assisted GSG 9 with the rescue at Mogadishu in 1977 (see below), while

Right: Two members of the counter-terrorist brotherhood pose for the camera. Spain's GEO is a highly trained and motivated anti-terrorist unit.

GSG 9's commander at the time, Ulrich Wegener, was consulted prior to the SAS assault on the Iranian Embassy in May 1980.

When GSG 9 was established in the early 1970s, the SAS and Mossad, the Israeli intelligence service, provided training and support facilities for the new unit. Now, instruction is given by GSG 9 to exchange officers from foreign CT units, such as the American FBI and Delta Force, Britain's SAS, GIGN and the Israeli Sayeret Mat'kal (the unit that spectacularly rescued the Israeli hostages being held at Entebbe in July 1976). These officers are attached to GSG 9 to exchange ideas on tactics and equipment, and many friendships are formed during these exchanges that can greatly ease many of the political problems that may arise when requests are subsequently made for international cooperation.

The SAS has strong links with other counter-terrorist units

Such is the goodwill between many CT units that offers of help are made without requests. During the planning phase for Operation 'Eagle Claw', for example, the abortive US mission to rescue American hostages in Iran, the CIA lacked human intelligence assets inside Iran. Wegener offered to infiltrate a team of GSG 9 operators, using the cover of a television team, into Tehran to obtain the intelligence needed to rescue the hostages. However, for reasons that are still not clear, the offer was rejected.

The SAS has strong links with other CT units. At Hereford, the Operations Planning and Intelligence cell, nicknamed the 'Kremlin', keeps tabs on more than 300 active terrorist cells currently operating worldwide. It is thus essential to maintain links with other counter-terrorist organisations throughout the world. Therefore, exchange officers with the SAS will include men from GIGN, GSG 9, the FBI, NOCS, Delta Force and GEO, plus those from many Third World units.

The SAS has often been called upon to train foreign units in all aspects of hostage-rescue and counter-terrorism. The Italians are a case in point. In 1978, the Italian Red Brigades terrorists killed former Prime Minister Aldo Moro after trial by a so-called 'people's tribunal'. While the hunt for Moro was being conducted, the Special Air Service was helping the Italians

to create a specialist anti-terrorist unit – NOCS. The Italians benefited greatly, and today, NOCS is the premier Italian intervention unit and consists of 50 police officers drawn mainly from the Carabinieri and trained at the Abbosanta Police Training Centre on Sardinia.

One way of illustrating just how good the SAS is among the CT fraternity, and the high esteem it is held in among the other members of the CT community, is to list those CT units the SAS has helped to establish. The list is impressive: GEO, NOCS, Delta Force, Singapore's Police Tactical Unit, Philippines' Aviation Security Commando, Pakistan's Special Services Group, Sri Lanka's Army Commando Squadron, Malaysia's Special Strike Unit,

Bahrain's U-Group, Jordan's Special Forces Battalion, Oman's Sultan's Special Force and Morocco's GIGN. This represents over 10 per cent of all the CT formations in the world which have been set up in the image of their creator. No other unit can claim such a record.

At the end of the day, however, actual operations are the acid test of whether a unit is up to the job. This was uppermost in the minds of the senior officers of the SAS in the 1970s. They had prepared the Regiment for hostage-rescue missions and believed their men were ready for any eventuality. But training isn't everything, and there was a nagging doubt that perhaps there had been flaws in the preparations. The subsequent rescue of civilian held by terrorists at the Iranian Embassy in London in 1980 allayed such fears. So how good is the SAS when compared to other units?

Leroy Thompson in his book *The Rescuers* devotes a chapter to evaluating the top hostage-rescue units in the world, with marks awarded for command and control, training, personnel, weapons and equipment, intelligence and versatility. Units are evaluated in each category by marks out of five, and the SAS is the top unit with 30 marks, a perfect score. Behind the SAS comes, in order, GSG 9, GIGN, the Australian SAS and the Israelis.

The Americans have a lot of work to do to repair their image

Coming from an American this is praise indeed, and the facts would seem to back Thompson up: in the last 20 years there have been only a handful of hostage-rescue operations. These include the rescue of French schoolchildren from Somali terrorists by GIGN (February 1976), the raid on Entebbe by the Israelis (July 1976), the ending of the train hijack by Dutch Marines (June 1977), GSG 9's assault at Mogadishu (October 1977), the French Foreign Legion's intervention in Kolwezi (May 1978), and the SAS assault on the Iranian Embassy (May 1980). The Americans are notably absent from this list, and for good reason. Delta Force's attempts at hostage-rescue have been spectacular failures. For example, the attempted rescue of

US hostages being held in Tehran, Iran, in 1980, codenamed Operation 'Eagle Claw', did not even get close to the actual hostages before it had to be aborted, the Americans leaving a lot of their equipment (and some personnel) as charred debris in the desert. Similarly, the heliborne assault on Richmond Hill prison during the invasion of Grenada (see By Air Chapter) was characterised by errors that mitigate against calling Delta an elite unit. The Americans have a lot of work to do to repair their image.

At Mogadishu the body of the pilot was dumped on the tarmac

Of the aforementioned successful operations, the SAS took part in the two most successful (successful in the sense of total number of hostages rescued compared to those killed): Mogadishu and the Iranian Embassy. These two operations will be examined in more detail in order to analyse how what are the world's top two hostage-rescue units, the British SAS and GSG 9, operate.

On 13 October 1977, four Palestinian terrorists (two men and two women) hijacked a Lufthansa Boeing 737 passenger airliner en route from the Balearic Islands to Germany. Their leader was the terrorist Zohair Akache, self-styled 'Captain Mahmoud', and they demanded the immediate release of 11 Baader-Meinhof terrorists in jail in West Germany. On board the aircraft were five crew and 86 passengers.

GSG 9 was put on immediate alert, and subsequent liaisons between the British and West German governments concerning the affair resulted in two SAS soldiers, Major Alastair Morrison and Sergeant Barry Davies, flying to Dubai (where the hijacked aircraft first landed) to assist the 30-strong GSG 9 team, which was commanded by Ulrich Wegener. The SAS soldiers had with them a quantity of Hereford-made stun grenades, which would prove invaluable later on.

Eventually the aircraft landed at Mogadishu, Somalia, after a diversion to Aden. In Aden Mahmoud had shot and killed the aircraft's captain, Jurgen Schuman, for supposedly secretly communicating with the security forces. At

Mogadishu the body was dumped on the runway. Accompanying this obscene gesture was a threat to kill the rest of the hostages if his demands were not met.

To gain time, negotiators informed him that 11 terrorists were being freed from West German prisons, and so Mahmoud magnanimously decided to delay blowing up the aircraft until 0230 hours on 18 October 1977. This was irrelevant, however, as Wegener had already decided to storm the aircraft, an operation codenamed 'Magic Fire'.

The SAS, on the face of it, had a slightly easier task when six armed terrorists of the Democratic Revolutionary Front for the Liberation of Arabistan (a region of Iran peopled not by Iranians but by ethnic Arabs) seized 22

hostages at the Iranian Embassy in London on the morning of 30 April 1980. The Regiment did not have to send a team to another country to effect a rescue, and it also had the co-operation of the authorities (something GSG 9 did not receive from the government on Yemen). As soon as the hostages were taken in London the terrorists issued their demands, which had a depressing familiarity about them: the release of 92 Arabs being held in Iranian jails and a safe passage for themselves once this had been achieved. If these demands were not met, the hostages would start dying.

Below: Practising assault drills. The soldier on the right is armed with an MP5K submachine gun, a shortened version of the venerable MP5.

As soon as the incident took place, an SAS Special Projects Team was despatched from Hereford. Codenamed 'Red Team', it consisted of a captain and 24 troopers from B Squadron. The building was already sealed off by the time the soldiers arrived, and police negotiators were in the process of trying to wear the terrorists down (taking Churchill's maxim that 'it is better to jaw, jaw than war, war' to the limit). The SAS took no part in these talks – they are the veiled threat in the background during any talks.

Like all hostage-rescue units, the SAS has an 'immediate assault plan' during any hostage situation, whereby the men can go in at a moment's notice should the the crisis deteriorate. This would have meant storming the building without knowing the precise whereabouts of the hostages – a blueprint for a large number of casualties. Fortunately, this turned out to be unnecessary, and so the SAS set about formulating a 'deliberate assault plan', which would hopefully be implemented at the time and choosing of the SAS.

As the negotiations went on at Princes Gate, another SAS team, codenamed 'Blue Team' (25 men) arrived during the afternoon of 2 May. The building and its surroundings were scrutinised by the SAS. Microphones were installed in the walls and down the chimneys to ascertain the location of the hostages and terrorists, and a full-scale model of the embassy was constructed by Army engineers at Regent's Park Barracks. At a higher

Below: History in the making: just after 1900 hours on 5 May 1980. Operation 'Nimrod', the SAS assault on the Iranian Embassy, gets under way.

Above: SAS soldiers on the roof of the Iranian Embassy on 5 May 1980. Their operation to free the hostages has entered elite forces folklore.

level, Prime Minister Margaret Thatcher consulted with senior members of the Ministry of Defence, MI5, MI6 and the SAS – meetings known as the Cabinet Office Briefing Room (COBRA) – at which it was decided that no concessions would be made to the terrorists.

The same decision had been taken by the West German government in 1977. At Mogadishu Ulrich Wegener, liaising closely with the Somalis, closed off the area around the Boeing 737 with Somali commandos. At 1730 hours on 17 October, an aircraft belonging to Lufthansa landed at Mogadishu and stopped 2000m from the hijacked aircraft. Inside was the GSG 9

assault team, armed with Mauser 66 sniper rifles, MP5 submachine guns, Smith & Wesson 38 Special and Heckler & Koch P9 handguns, and equipped with night sights and armour vests. When it was dark the GSG 9 reconnaissance and sniper teams moved into position. Using infrared equipment, they studied the aircraft and relayed their findings back to Wegener in the control tower. Mahmoud and another terrorist were confirmed as being in the cockpit, though the whereabouts of the other terrorists were not known.

The plan was to light a diversionary fire in front of the aircraft, which it was hoped would induce the terrorists into the cockpit. Then, four GSG 9 assault teams, one led by Wegener himself, would storm the aircraft via front and rear door and emergency exits over the wings.

The SAS plan at Princes Gate was fairly simple: 'Red Team' would enter and clear the top half of the embassy, while 'Blue Team' cleared the lower half. As support, the teams had a host of snipers positioned in the surrounding buildings. However, unlike at Mogadishu, the SAS did not know the exact whereabouts of the hostages. It was originally thought that they were being held in an office at the rear of the building, but this would turn out to be incorrect.

The decision to assault the embassy was taken when the terrorists killed the embassy's chief press officer, Abbas Lavasani, and dumped his body on the pavement outside during the early evening of 5 May. At 1907 hours, therefore, the SAS commander, Lieutenant-Colonel Mike Rose, took control and implemented Operation 'Nimrod', the codename for the SAS rescue mission.

The signal to go – 'London Bridge' – was given

On the roof 'Red Team' was ready: two teams of four men would abseil down to the second-floor balcony at the back of the building, another group would assault the third floor, while more men would enter through the skylight on the fourth floor. The signal to go – 'London Bridge' – was given and the men abseiled down, only for the commander to get snagged on his harness. As the others tried to help him, a window was smashed by a boot. The element of surprise, so vital for hostage rescues, was seemingly lost. Thus the SAS soldiers rushed frantically to reach the hostages before they were killed, though subsequent published memoirs of those who took part (notably *Soldier I*) reveal that assault team members believed as they were going in that they were too late to save the hostages. Fortunately they were wrong.

At Mogadishu, GSG 9 faced one major problem. Assaulting an aircraft is extremely difficult: the hostages and terrorists are in a confined space, calling for a high degree of accuracy with weapons if hostage deaths are to be avoided. Aircraft contain very inflammable materials (foam seats, carpets, oil and aviation fuel in the wings), therefore explosive charges

have to be used with care. In addition, entry points are small and can therefore be easily defended. Thus surprise is absolutely vital.

Fortunately for GSG 9, surprise was total as the men approached the aircraft from behind and took up position under the wings. Once inside the aircraft, Wegener would shout the command 'heads down', which would be the signal for his men to shoot anyone left standing (he assumed, correctly, that the hostages would duck down on his command).

The SAS used explosive charges at Princes Gate

At 0005 hours on 18 October, as the terrorists watched the diversionary fire, rubber-coated alloy ladders were placed silently against the sides of the aircraft and explosive charges laid against the entry points. The two SAS men, Morrison and Davies, prepared their stun grenades. Then the charges were set off and the stun grenades thrown inside the cabin.

The SAS also used explosive charges at the Iranian Embassy in Princes Gate to blow in the windows on the first-floor balcony, though not before they had to yell at one of the hostages, Sim Harris, to back away from the window inside the building. The hostages were being held in the telex room on the second floor, and the terrorists started to shoot them as soon as the assault got under way. Thus it was a race against time, but it is to the SAS's enormous credit that only one hostage was killed before they reached the room.

The SAS meticulously cleared the building using standard room-clearance drills: shoot off the lock, kick in the door, throw in a stun grenade, than enter and clear the room. The weapons skills of the individual troopers manifested themselves as the terrorists were dealt with one by one: the leader shot dead on the first-floor balcony, two killed in the telex room, one killed in the hallway near the front door, and one shot dead in an office at the rear of the building.

At Mogadishu the GSG 9 officers put down the terrorists speedily. In the cockpit Mahmoud was hit several times by bullets from a Smith &

Above: The aftermath at Mogadishu. A blood-splattered terrorist lies dead and the hostages are safe, all courtesy of GSG 9.

killing the terrorists, saving the lives of the hostages, only for them to die of suffocation or burns because evacuation procedures are too slow). At Princes Gate parts of the building had been set on fire during the assault, and all the rooms were beginning to fill with smoke and CS gas as the SAS troopers began to evacuate the occupants. This they did at speed and with little regard for personal comfort, bundling the hostages out onto the embassy lawn, where they were bound and laid face-down. They were then examined, and the surviving terrorist was found among them.

At Mogadishu the evacuation of the hostages began immediately

At Mogadishu the evacuation of the hostages began before all the terrorists had been dealt with, the fear of hidden explosive charges being uppermost in the minds of the GSG 9 officers (the threat of fire was very real, which if it had broken out would have resulted in the cabin filling with choking smoke). Three passengers had been wounded but none killed – it had been a superb operation.

Mogadishu and Princes Gate are examples of highly trained hostage-rescue units in action, operations which have yet to be bettered. Their success was the direct result of intensive training, slick drills, good command and control and the proper choice of equipment, the culmination of years of training and research into what equipment and tactics to use. They are also a reminder of the one ingredient all hostage-rescue units must possess if they are to rescue hostages alive from the clutches of armed terrorists: luck.

There is one more point that should be made with regard to hostage-rescue: no SAS operation has resulted in large-scale loss of life among hostages. This is an important point to make, for there is a line of thought that maintains that it is acceptable that 10 per cent or more of the hostages will be killed during an assault. For the SAS this is unacceptable. However, only if you are the best trained and equipped CT unit – the best bar none – can you set such standards.

Wesson handgun, but still managed to throw two grenades, which exploded harmlessly under seats (the poor stopping power of the Smith & Wesson could have fatally compromised the operation). He was finished off by a burst from an MP5. The other terrorist in the cockpit had been shot in the head by Wegener.

In the passenger compartment one female terrorist had been encountered and shot dead immediately, but the other woman took cover in a toilet and opened fire, slightly wounding a GSG 9 trooper. She was then engaged with gunfire and seriously wounded – the aircraft was now finally secure.

One of the most important procedures in a rescue is the evacuation of the hostages after the terrorists have been neutralised (after all, the rescue of the hostages is the only reason the team attacks in the first place; there is no point in

COUNTER-INSURGENCY

Counter-insurgency warfare has been important in over 100 conflicts since 1945. What is involved in the waging of a counter-insurgency campaign? And which unit has proved to be the most effective?

A comprehensive account of all the counter-insurgency (COIN) campaigns since 1945 and the participation of elite units in them would fill a large book, and is therefore impossible to present in one chapter. Thus we will compare one of the most successful COIN campaigns since World War II – the SAS campaign in Oman in the 1970s – with one of the most well known – the US Special Forces' Civilian Irregular Defense Group (CIDG) Program during the Vietnam War. But first, what is COIN warfare?

In the period of decolonisation following World War II, when the Western powers began to relinquish control, voluntarily or otherwise, of their empires, there occurred a number of insurgency wars. Their aim was simple: to drive out the colonial power by force. Because they did not have sizeable or well-armed armies, the insurgents adopted guerrilla tactics, and in the 1950s and 1960s, British soldiers fought against guerrillas in Kenya, Malaya, Borneo, Cyprus and Aden. The tool that the insurgents were in fact using to rid themselves of colonial rule (which Britain for one recognised was largely out-dated by this time) was revolutionary warfare.

SAS 'hearts and minds' in action. A medic treats locals in Oman. Simple medicine often won the trust and friendship of indigenous peoples, and proved invaluable to the counter-insurgency effort.

The theory of revolutionary warfare states that the revolutionaries rely on guerrilla warfare and subversion, not conventional warfare. The aim is to replace the existing government with one of their own choosing, and the alternative rulers collect taxes, conscripts and intelligence, all of which are used to erode the position of the legitimate government. The population is subverted, either by persuasion or terror, to the side of the guerrillas. Thus, areas theoretically under the control of the government are actually in the grip of the guerrillas. Conventional military efforts to destroy the revolutionaries are uneconomical and ineffective, and tend to further alienate the civil population, since the guerrillas invariably melt away in the face of superior firepower, and it is always civilians who are caught in the middle.

For a revolution to succeed, there has to be a large pool of civil discontent which the insurgents can tap. According to the US Army's

Above: US Green Beret-trained Montagnards line up prior to an expedition against the Viet Cong. Their weapons are M3 'grease guns'.

manual on guerrilla warfare: 'Resistance, rebellion or civil war begins in a nation where political, sociological, economic or religious division has occurred. Divisions of this nature are usually caused by a violation of rights or privileges, the oppression of one group by the dominant or occupying force, or the threat to the life and freedom of the populace. Resistance also may develop in a nation where the once welcomed liberators have failed to improve an intolerable social or economic situation. Resistance can also be deliberately inspired from external sources against an assumed grievance. Resistance can be active or passive. Passive resistance may be in the form of smouldering resentment which needs only leadership or a means of expression to mature to active resistance.'

However, the West, specifically the British and Americans, discovered that insurgents could be matched by specialist soldiers trained to fight the guerrillas on their own or to train indigenous forces to do so. There was also a recognition that these elite soldiers had to have the skills to win another battle – the battle for men's minds.

'Hearts and minds' concentrates on gaining the trust of the locals

In Britain, as a result of its campaign in Malaya, the SAS assumed a Counter Revolutionary Warfare (CRW) role, which is effectively the same as COIN warfare. They called it 'hearts and minds'. Originally devised by the Military High Commissioner in Malaya, General Sir Gerald Templar, to defeat the communist insurgents during the 'Emergency' of 1948-60, it subsequently became an integral part of the SAS's COIN warfare methods. 'Hearts and minds' concentrates on gaining the trust of the local inhabitants by learning their language, customs and sharing their lifestyle. During the campaign in Borneo (1963-66), for example, SAS soldiers lived with the natives for months at a time, assisting them in their everyday needs and providing medical care. In this way the locals learned to trust the SAS and gave them information on the enemy – the months of patience, tact and courtesy were well rewarded.

The Americans trained their Special Forces for COIN warfare, and today these are the only two elite units that have a dedicated COIN role. This is reflected in their training (see Selection and Training Chapter) and use on operations (see Operational Tactics Chapter). This is an important point, because COIN is not just a matter of military tactics and weapons skills. Units such as Spetsnaz in Afghanistan, the French Foreign Legion in Algeria in the 1950s and 1960s, the Royal Marines in Borneo in the 1960s and the SEALs in Vietnam, all achieved tactical successes against insurgents. But they were not trained to deny the 'sea' to the guerrilla 'fish', something that is so important if a COIN campaign is to succeed. This requires civil aid programmes, which in turn requires medical and linguistic skills, both of which are far more important than

weapons skills. So how were these specialist skills put into practice in Oman and South Vietnam?

As a maritime nation, Britain signed a treaty of friendship with the Sultan of Muscat in 1789, which gave the East India Company commercial rights in exchange for Britain's providing the sultan with the protection of the Royal Navy. The treaty worked well: Oman was a sea-faring nation which was threatened by pirates; the Royal Navy gradually eradicated them. For their part, the British were happy to continue the relationship. In the twentieth century a new element arose: oil.

Because of Oman's position, situated on the southeast corner of the Arabian peninsula, the West's oil supplies could be interfered with or halted by a hostile regime there. The British, smarting from their experience in Aden, were keen to avoid this. They had supported the sultan, Said bin Taimur, in the late 1950s, when the SAS conducted the Jebel Akhdar operation. However, the oppressive policies of the sultan resulted in rebellion flaring up once again, and again the British were called upon for help.

Dhofar was severely repressed by Sultan Said bin Taimur

This time the rebellion was in the province of Dhofar, in the southwest of the country, which is dominated by the massive Jebel Dhofar. The area's population of 500,000 was severely repressed by Said bin Taimur, and this resulted in armed resistance breaking out in 1962, albeit in a half-hearted fashion. The Dhofar Liberation Front (DLF) was hardly the most radical revolutionary organisation, emphasising as it did traditionalism, the Moslem religion and the tribal structure. Its fighters were, for the most part, poorly armed and equipped, and the deployment of 1000 men of the Sultan's Armed Forces (SAF) to the area initially contained the rebellion.

To the west of Oman lay the People's Democratic Republic of Yemen (PDRY), which gave refuge to the radical People's Front for the Liberation of the Occupied Arabian Gulf (PFLOAG), a communist group that received weapons and money from both the Soviet Union and China. The PFLOAG suggested a merger

Above: At the desert airstrip of Ibri, Oman, soldiers of A Squadron, 22 SAS, unload supplies to assist the local Dhofari economy and war effort.

with the DLF, though the latter was at first reluctant, finding little merit in the atheist ideology of the larger group. However, money and modern weapons were powerful persuaders, and the DLF eventually agreed.

The larger group quickly swallowed up the DLF, and well-organised communist cells started to spring up on the Jebel Dhofar. For its part, the SAF didn't have the training to conduct a COIN war. In addition, the Sultan of Oman's Air Force didn't help the situation. For example, there was little liaison between the army and air force, and if a patrol encountered a force of guerrillas, air support would arrive only after the action, when the aircraft would usually bomb the nearest village. This, not unnaturally, alienated the civilian population still further. By 1970 the PFLOAG had control of the whole Jebel Dhofar and the Sultan was staring defeat in the face.

Alienation of the local population was also a factor in the Central Highlands of Vietnam in the early 1960s. The area was populated by a large number of Montagnard aborigines, who had a distinct culture and were highly superstitious. They were regarded as savages by the Vietnamese, and viewed as a potential threat by the South Vietnamese government. In view of this the Montagnards, unsurprisingly, were hostile to the Vietnamese.

The South Vietnamese, however, could not afford to leave the Montagnards alone, for the government of President Diem was in trouble: the communist Viet Cong (VC) were at work in the Central Highlands and were recruiting people to their cause. The situation resembled that in Oman 10 years later: the authorities in the region were on the verge of defeat – something had to be done.

The response came from the US backers of the South Vietnamese. The Green Berets realised that the answer lay in civil aid activities that would act as an incentive to the Montagnards to support the South Vietnamese regime – i.e. a COIN campaign was called for. Something needed to be done quickly: in late 1961 the CIA reckoned that the Viet Cong controlled around half of the country's western highlands.

Likewise in Oman. The SAS regimental commander at the time, Lieutenant-Colonel Johnny Watts, came to the conclusion that a COIN programme was the only way that defeat could be averted in Dhofar, but he also realised that it would be ineffective without the removal of Said bin Taimur. An SAS team had been in Oman since 1969 training the sultan's forces, but with Said bin Taimur still ruling there was no scope for a COIN campaign. On 23 July 1970, all that changed.

On that date the sultan's son, Qaboos, who had been under virtual house arrest for seven years because he was viewed as being too liberal by his father (Qaboos had been educated in the West), overthrew his father in a palace coup. Within days the new sultan, protected by SAS bodyguards, had announced a general amnesty and plans for civil aid throughout Oman. Watts' plan now seemed much more realistic.

The 'Five Fronts' campaign was designed to win the Dhofari war

Within hours of the coup an SAS team landed in Dhofar. It was officially known as a British Army Training Team (BATT), so it could be denied by the British government that any British troops were actively engaged in Oman. The regime at this time was in a bad way: the sultan's forces had been driven from the mountains and were restricted to the coastal towns of Salalah, Rakyut, Taqa and Mirbat. The Dhofaris would have to be won back, therefore Watts devised his 'Five Fronts' campaign to achieve this.

The 'Five Fronts' campaign, a logical extension of the proven 'Hearts and Minds' concept, was an ingenious SAS plan to win the war in Dhofar. There were five aspects to the campaign: the SAS would establish an intelligence cell to assess the overall situation; an information cell would be set up to ensure the population was fully informed about the government's civil aid programme, as well as to counter

the propaganda of the enemy's Radio Aden; an effort would be made by SAS and government medics to improve the health of the local populace; veterinary services would be made available to the Dhofaris; and the SAS would raise Dhofari units to fight for the sultan. The plan relied on the support of the new sultan, and his endorsement led to its implementation. Its ultimate aim was to give the Omanis the skills to allow them to do everything themselves.

The general betterment of the locals' living standards was also behind the CIDG Program in Vietnam. The first involvement of the US Army Special Forces in the Central Highlands began in December 1961, with the establishment of the

Below: A US Special Forces sergeant gives instruction to CIDG Program volunteers in the use of the 60mm mortar.

pilot Village Defense Program at Buon Enao village in Darlac Province.

The village population of 400 included many VC supporters, mainly because the Vietnamese government had failed to protect the villagers. Thus through fear they had no choice but to support the enemy. In addition, the government had stopped medical and educational aid as a result of the VC activity in the area – this hardly endeared the government to the villagers.

During two weeks of discussions the villagers agreed to erect a fence around the village to show their support for the programme, to build housing for a training centre and a dispensary for medical aid, and to set up an intelligence system to control movement into and out of the village. Special Forces Detachment A-113 trained the volunteer village defenders, and the US soldiers

Above: SAS language skills are integral to a counter-insurgency campaign. Here, troopers converse with bedouin in Oman in the early 1970s.

distributed supplies and medicine to the locals. The soldiers were always very careful to show tact and to respect local customs.

Once the programme at Buon Enao had been established, Green Beret A Team detachments expanded their operations. They started to make visits to other villages, taking with them a wide range of supplies and medicines, and encouraged the settlements to join the programme. Before a village could be accepted into the programme the village chief was consulted and had to confirm that everyone in the village would participate in the programme and that a sufficient number of people would volunteer to train to be a part of the village protection force. By August 1962 five A Teams were deployed in the CIDG Program, with over 200 villages under their protection.

In Oman, the SAS team at Salalah conveyed the sultan's amnesty in the late summer of 1970. In September a full SAS squadron arrived, enabling the work of the BATTs to be stepped up. The task was still daunting, but it was alleviated somewhat in the same month when a group of PFLOAG rebels, led by Salim Mubarak, fought their way off the Jebel Dhofar and surrendered to the government.

The defection of Salim Mubarak was a godsend to the SAS

Though the PFLOAG had control of most of the jebel, its methods were often counter-productive. Its hardline communist ideology meant that the tribal structure in place among the inhabitants of Dhofar was anathema to it, and so the movement endeavoured to destroy this traditionalism. Children were forcibly removed from their parents and sent for schooling in the Yemen, old men were tortured for refusing to deny the existence of God, and young men were sent to China and the Soviet Union for training in guerrilla warfare. The full panoply of 'people's power' was established on the jebel. For example, people's courts were set up that dished out revolutionary justice: innocent people were executed on the slightest pretext. Such techniques worked for a while, but the Dhofaris are a proud people who have a strong belief in Islam. The communists' heavy handedness and denial of the existence of God offended many and played into the hands of the government.

The defection of Salim Mubarak was a godsend to the SAS. He was a hardened DLF fighter who was the second-in-command of the rebels' Eastern Area, and was therefore a figure of some influence and power. In discussions with Major Tony Jeapes of 22 SAS, Mubarak suggested the formation of anti-rebel groups, and the idea was put into practice. Mubarak had brought two dozen men with him, and these formed the core of a *firqat* irregular unit. It would be called the *Firqat Salahadin* and would

be drawn from several tribes. The SAS began training the men at Mirbat.

COIN programmes require a great deal of patience and skill on the part of the special forces trainers, and both Green Berets and SAS troopers came near to exasperation as they wrestled with the problems of dealing with alien cultures which were unused to Western ways. In Oman, for example, there was initially some friction between the *firqat* members and the SAS. The Dhofaris believe that all things come from God, therefore it is inappropriate being grateful to men for things that are given to you, since it is God's will that you should have it. Also, they hold the view that you should ask for anything you want – if it is God's will that you should have it, then you will get it.

This outlook meant the *firqat* were never grateful for anything they received, and didn't hesitate to demand whatever they wanted. When the *firqat* units were first being formed, the SAS had no choice but to listen to individual demands and requests, however unreasonable, so as not to offend. When the trust between the SAS and *firqats* had been forged in battle, the SAS were able to reduce the amount of pestering by insisting that all requests go through *firqat* leaders.

The expansion of the CIDG Program meant new tribes were trained

The Green Berets training the Montagnards didn't have many initial problems with culture clashes. Though the tribesmen were unused to Western affluence, liberal quantities of arms, money, medicines and other supplies meant the hill people were quick to accept the incentives. Once a group had set civic action in progress in an area, detachments from the US Special Forces and the Vietnamese Special Forces (the Luc Luong Dac Biet, or LLDB) would begin military training. Defensive positions would be erected around villages, and the men would receive training in the use of the M1 carbine and the M3 'grease gun' submachine gun. Other topics taught included basic tactics and radio operation. By the end of 1963, the Green Berets, with the aid of the LLDB, had trained 18,000 strike force troops and over 43,000 hamlet militiamen.

It had always been envisaged that the CIDG Program would be a part of offensive operations against the VC, and from early 1963 there was a subtle shift in the employment of 'cidgees' as they began aggressive patrolling, searching out the enemy and laying ambushes. Thus, a force originally created to protect its own villages was adopting new roles.

The rapid expansion of the CIDG Program meant new tribes were trained by the Green Berets, including ethnic Cambodians and Nungs. This created a degree of new inter-tribal hostility, but worse was the continuing enmity between the mountain people and the South Vietnamese. This was to have dire consequences in 1964 (see below).

Below: SAS troopers with *firqat* soldiers during an offensive against the *adoo*. Firqat units fought well in combat if used correctly.

The SAS had few such problems in Dhofar, where things progressed rapidly after the civil aid programme got under way. SAS teams established clinics for the people and their animals, and advanced drilling equipment was brought in from Britain to bore new wells or open old ones that had been sealed on the orders of Said bin Taimur. A Civil Aid Department was established which set in motion many schemes, such as transporting prefabricated buildings to Dhofar to act as schools, clinics and shops.

Between September 1970 and March 1971, 200 enemy guerrillas, *adoo* as they were known, surrendered to the government, and were formed into *firqat* units by the SAS. But the latter realised that a victory was needed to convince waverers that government forces were now able to defeat the rebels. The *firqat* were not conventional infantry as such; rather, they were reconnaissance troops who collected

Above: Camp Polei Kleng, one of the many US Special Forces fortified positions that were constructed under the CIDG Program.

intelligence. Nevertheless, the SAS had to prove to the *adoo* and Dhofaris, as well as the *firqat* recruits themselves, that they could hold their own in battle. Thus, they needed to be blooded.

In his excellent book *SAS: Operation Oman*, Tony Jeapes, who as an SAS officer was instrumental in establishing the *Firqat Salahadin*, wrote: 'When a unit is being "blooded" for the first time it must be successful or their confidence may be irretrievably destroyed.' It was therefore important that the whereabouts of the blooding be carefully chosen. The coastal town of Sudh was selected as the place where the *firqat* were to be tested. SAS and *firqat* were off-loaded from a boat – 100 men on an important mission. The actual assault was a disappointment: there were no *adoo* in the town and it was quickly taken. Nevertheless, the first, all-important, victory had been achieved – there was no turning back.

Sudh resulted in an expansion of the number of *firqat* units, which was excellent news for the counter-insurgency effort. Training the *firqat* could be infuriating, however, especially when it came to small arms. Being former *adoo* fighters,

they were used to Soviet AK-47 automatic assault rifles. However, when they joined the *firqats* they were given British Self-Loading Rifles (SLRs). The SLR is an excellent weapon, but the British version did not fire full-automatic, and it was heavier than the AK-47. This caused grumblings among the *firqat*, until the SAS solved it by proving that the SLR was a much better weapon. On the range the *firqats* were allowed to shoot both guns, with the result that individuals achieved much better results with the semi-automatic fire of the SLR. This ended the complaints.

This was not something the Green Berets encountered in their dealings with the Montagnards: the South Vietnamese had disarmed them. Therefore, they were glad to receive arms to enable them to defend their villages. The programme grew apace. However, the expansion caused problems: there was hostility between the different tribes, and the problems between the Montagnards and the South Vietnamese remained. This hostility resulted in the Montagnard uprising in September 1964.

The rebellion was in the Ban Me Thuot area of the central highlands, and began during the night of 19/20 September, when the strike force components of five CIDG camps killed 11 LLDB soldiers and moved north in trucks to seize the Ban Me Thuot radio station and a key bridge. This was the signal for other Montagnards units to kill South Vietnamese personnel and march on Ban Me Thuot. This episode culminated in Montagnard forces and the South Vietnamese 23rd Division squaring up to each other outside the town on 20 September. Deft negotiating on the part of the Green Berets averted wholesale bloodshed, and the rebellion was ended. The South Vietnamese instituted a few token changes, but the distrust would not go away. The strike forces were developed further: Mobile Strike Forces were established, to be used in raids and sabotage missions, so-called 'Blackjack' Operations. By 1967, the CIDG camps were being constructed as 'fighting camps' designed to withstand enemy attack, and they were defended by machine guns and mortars.

Lympne was captured, to be followed by five days of fighting

The CIDG Program circumvented both the corrupt South Vietnamese system and US Army bureaucracy. CIDG camps and Green Berets were supplied from forward bases in the Corps Tactical Combat Zones, or from the US Army Counter-Insurgency Support Office at Okinawa. The Special Forces supply network also provided special equipment, such as foreign weapons for clandestine operations.

The need to take the war to the enemy was also appreciated by the SAS in Oman. Sudh had been a victory, but the *adoo* were still a force to be reckoned with, especially on the jebel. Therefore, Watts, the SAS commander, decided to launch an offensive onto the Jebel Dhofar. In October 1971, he assembled a force of 100 SAS, 250 SAF, a few northern tribesmen and five *firqat* (300 men) – in all some 800 troops. The

mission was designed to establish permanent government positions on the jebel.

The first part of the operation began on 2 October, when SAS soldiers and some *firqat* captured the old airstrip at Lympne after a gruelling march. Reinforcements were flown in using the airstrip, though Watts then decided that the airstrip at Jibjat was better suited to his needs; it was captured on 3 October. Five days of fierce fighting for the plateau then ensued. Watts divided the SAS into two groups, each one accompanied by *firqat*, and ordered them to advance down the western and eastern sides of the Wadi Darbat. This resulted in the *adoo* being cleared off the plateau.

The *firqat* stopped fighting and decided to observe Ramadan

At this point the *firqat* decided to stop fighting and observe the religious festival of Ramadan. As this meant they were not allowed to eat or drink between dawn and dusk, their military effectiveness was drastically reduced. Watts was enraged and had to pull his forces back to a place called 'White City', from where his force had to beat off a fierce *adoo* assault.

During November Watts continued operations, though the *firqat* again proved difficult: they demanded that their animals be brought off the jebel and transported to a government-organised market, or they would stop fighting. This request was eventually carried out. Despite these setbacks, By the end of 1971, Watts had established an Omani government presence on the jebel, which left the coastal plain and its towns under government control. In addition, 700 Dhofaris were now fighting in *firqat*, and the coastal plain was free of *adoo*. The PFLOAG attack and subsequent defeat at Mirbat in July 1972 (see Weapons Skills Chapter) was the turning point of the war in Dhofar. The civil aid programmes grew apace, and large numbers of Dhofaris began to defect to the government, the credibility of the PFLOAG having been dealt a fatal blow (the Soviet Union and China had also begun to withdraw their support). By 1975 the rebels had been pushed back to the Yemeni border, and the war was all but over.

Above: At a remote CIDG camp in South Vietnam, a Green Beret-manned 107mm mortar opens up against a Viet Cong attack.

In Vietnam, the Montagnards proved their worth during the Tet Offensive of January 1968, which gained them respect with the South Vietnamese forces. This was just as well, as the CIDG Program was being turned over to the control of the the South Vietnamese under President Nixon's policy of 'Vietnamization'. By early 1970 it had been decided to end the programme altogether and absorb the CIDG units into the South Vietnamese Army, and by the end of the year US Army Special Forces participation in the scheme had been brought to an end.

So how effective had the SAS and Green Berets been in their COIN programmes? Overall both programmes had been successful. In Vietnam, the CIDG Program made a real contribution to curbing communist insurgency, and compared with the SAS effort in Oman had been more successful in terms of number of people won over. The Green Berets had mobilised the tribal groups in remote areas and organised them into camp forces capable of defeating the VC. Despite the reluctance and sometimes hostility of the South Vietnamese regime, the 5th Special Forces Group had trained camp personnel to patrol North Vietnamese infiltration routes and bases, monitor borders and serve in battle as infantry.

In Vietnam China supported the North Vietnamese and VC

If there was a problem with the CIDG Program it was that the Special Forces performed the 'hearts and minds' aspect of their mission too well. The various tribes and ethnic minorities readily gave their loyalty to the Green Berets, but it was never extended so wholeheartedly to the government of South Vietnam or its servants. But to be fair, it would have been impossible for the Green Berets to change the attitude of the South Vietnamese towards the Montagnards.

A major reason for the eventual victory in Oman was that the major power in the region, Saudi Arabia, was pro-Western. This contrasts sharply with the situation in Vietnam. There, the major player in the area, China, was staunchly anti-Western. This went a long way to securing the eventual victory of the North Vietnamese and VC. This point is pertinent to all COIN campaigns: there is a limit to what elite teams can do in the long term if the major power in the region backs the insurgents.

Oman was a victory that came relatively cheaply, at least as far as the British government was concerned: 12 SAS soldiers killed during six years of war. For the Regiment, it was yet more proof, if any were needed, that its unique skills could achieve success out of all proportion to numbers committed if used correctly and imaginatively. For the West, what price could be put on uninterrupted oil supplies? It was a question that never had to be answered.

OPERATIONAL TACTICS

How do elite units, such as the SAS, SEALs and Green Berets, operate on the tactical level? And which one has the best blend of skills, firepower and flexibility?

P revious chapters have examined the specific skills and insertion techniques that are the hallmark of soldiers of the world's major elite formations, such as proficiency with different types of weapons, ability to survive and fight in various hostile environments, use of vehicles, small boats and aircraft, and so on. We have compared the men of the various SAS units with other elite soldiers, notably those men in units that are in the premier league of special forces organisations, such as the US Navy SEALs and US Army Green Berets.

However, elite soldiers do not fight alone; they work as part of a team, a small-sized tactical unit. But what size are these teams, which possess the most firepower, the widest diversity of skills and the greatest flexibility? We will compare the SAS with the Australian SAS, the Green Berets, the Royal Marines, Spetsnaz, the US Rangers and the SEALs to answer these questions, and to decide, when all the strands are drawn together, which is the best in the world.

Our starting point is the actual size of elite unit tactical teams. At their lowest level, all armies are composed of small

Victory does not necessarily go to the side that has the big battalions. Small-sized special forces teams invariably pack a lot of firepower and contain a multitude of skills.

Above: David Stirling's ideas being put into practice: an SAS team returns from an operation behind enemy lines in North Africa in World War II.

units that work together on the battlefield towards a common goal: the defeat of the enemy. Thus, four or five eight- or 10-man infantry sections will make up a platoon, while three or four platoons will compose a company. In turn, around four companies combine to form an infantry battalion and so on. In armoured units, the smallest tactical group is the three- or four-man crew of a main battle tank. Usually, four tanks compose a troop, five troops a squadron and five squadrons a regiment. Whatever the arm of service, therefore, men are trained to fight in small tactical teams that form a part of larger units.

Elite soldiers are also trained to fight in small units. In this they are no different from conventional outfits. However, there is a difference in how special forces teams are used in wartime and the blend of skills present in each individual unit. It is the task of conventional troops to defeat enemy forces on the battlefield, combining infantry, artillery, armour and aircraft to destroy the opposition's units and formations, seize and hold territory, and generally degrade the enemy's ability to wage war. To this end, massive, overwhelming firepower and immense supplies of fuel and ammunition, technologically advanced weaponry and signalling equipment, plus access to a large pool of reinforcements of both men and material, are crucial elements in achieving victory on the modern battlefield (witness the 1991 Gulf War between the UN and Iraq, and especially the total air superiority established by the Allies early on, which proved critical to the success of the subsequent land campaign).

Large-scale operations are anathema to elite units; rather, special forces teams are trained to infiltrate behind enemy lines, where they can cause disruption and destruction out of all proportion to their size. Special forces avoid contacts (unless conditions are extremely favourable), and do not attempt to hold ground – they operate in the shadows, seeking to exploit chinks in the enemy's armour. Their special talents are wasted on the conventional battlefield. But exactly how large, or small, are special forces teams?

The smallest tactical unit within the British SAS is the four-man patrol, which was invented by the Regiment's founder, David Stirling. During the early stages of World War II, commando-type operations tended to be relatively large-scale affairs, with often disastrous results. David Stirling took part in a number of ineffectual raids on the North African coast in 1941. These affairs convinced him that raids by small-sized units would be much more effective than the large-scale operations in which he had taken part. He summarised these thoughts in a memorandum while recovering from a parachute accident: 'The scale on which the Commando raids are planned, i.e. the number of troops employed on the one hand and the scale of equipment and facilities on the other, prejudices surprise beyond all possible compensating advantages in respect of the defensive and aggressive striking power afforded. Moreover, the Navy has to provide ships to lift the force

which results in the risking of naval units valuable out of all proportion even to a successful raid...It follows that 200 properly selected, trained and equipped men, organised into these sub-units, will be able to attack up to 10 different objectives at the same time on the same night as compared to only one objective using the current Commando technique.'

As a result of a combination of bluff and audacity, L Detachment, Special Air Service Brigade, was born. Stirling's original idea was to have five-man teams operating behind Axis lines in North Africa. He believed that this number would combine the minimum firepower requirements with the maximum possibilities of surprise. However, it was subsequently discovered that the number could be reduced to four men.

The four-man patrol endured, and today is the cornerstone of the Regiment's art of war.

Below: Australian SAS soldiers on exercise. The Australians favour five-man patrols for missions, not four as in the British SAS.

The SAS still believes that four is the ideal tactical number of men to maximise the chances of surprise, while at the same time having sufficient mobility and firepower. The four-man patrol is the building block upon which the British SAS is founded, and since World War II has proved itself to be a highly effective tactical formation. Currently, each SAS troop is made up of four four-man patrols, while four troops compose an SAS Sabre Squadron. How does the four-man patrol compare with the tactical units of other elite formations?

The Green Berets have as their basic module the 12-man A Team

The Australian SAS has the five-man patrol as the basic module. The Australian experience in Indonesia and Vietnam showed that the four-man patrol never really worked for them in combat. For example, for jungle warfare the British SAS developed the tactic of 'shoot and scoot', whereby a patrol would make a rapid withdrawal in the event of a contact with the enemy. However, if a man was hit he would have to make his own way to the emergency jungle rendezvous. This was not to the Australians' liking, and so their doctrine demanded another team member carry the wounded man to the helicopter landing zone. However, this reduced a four-man patrol's firepower to just two weapons – potentially fatal in a combat zone. In these circumstances it could experience severe difficulties in breaking contact, especially if the enemy attempted to out-flank the patrol, as the Viet Cong (VC) frequently did during the Vietnam War. Therefore the Australians adopted the five-man patrol.

American special forces units tend to deploy slightly larger tactical teams, a reflection of their generally larger resources and the specific roles of individual units within the US armed forces. The Rangers, which are in fact light infantry, employ six- or seven-man reconnaissance patrols or even larger squads, platoons and companies, though the larger units tend to be for missions of limited duration, or for direct action operations, such as quick strike and shock actions deep into enemy territory.

The Green Berets have as their basic module the 12-man A Team, composed of the following personnel: detachment commander (captain), executive officer (lieutenant), operations sergeant, assistant operations sergeant, heavy weapons leader, medical specialist, radio operator supervisor, chief radio operator, engineer sergeant, assistant medical NCO, chief radio operator and special forces engineer. The 12-man A Team is the basic training unit and the basic patrol composition during the move to and from the operational area. On operations, two, three or more Special Forces advisors may accompany an indigenous force of 10-20 men. In Vietnam, a large number of A Team personnel commanded and led indigenous forces numbering several hundred strong, which were often used as reaction forces or for other special missions.

US Army Special Forces are trainers: instruction is their primary operational tactic. They build up indigenous armies using their 30- or 60-day Master Program. Trained recruits become part of indigenous A Detachments which run their own Master Training Programs, which in turn produce more leaders and specialists. The Green Berets train foreign troops or partisans or militias with the aim of securing the Unconventional Warfare Operational Area (UWOA) and then extending it using ambushes, raids and interdiction. During operations they provide guidance, leadership and support, but their protégés do the majority of the fighting.

SEAL tactical unit size depends on the type of mission and insertion

The tactics are the same regardless of whether the Green Berets are fighting a conventional army with partisans, or fighting partisans on behalf of a friendly government and with a conventional army. In both cases the doctrine centres around 'terrain denial'. In addition, they may also train and support foreign conventional forces. During the 1991 Gulf War, for example, Green Berets were attached to Arab Coalition forces and taught the usual military skills, but the instruction that really made the difference was in close air support instruction given to Arab allied tactical units, which was coordinated and

controlled by attached US Special Forces advisors throughout the conflict.

Britain's Royal Marines employ the conventional tactical units of sections, platoons, companies and battalions (though they call the last-mentioned commandos). The more specialist sub-units within the Marines, such as the Special Boat Service (SBS) also deploy four-man patrols, which may combine into eight-man or larger teams for operations.

US Navy SEAL teams are usually divided into platoons, detachments and reconnaissance

Above: An SAS trooper in Borneo in the early 1960s searches for the enemy. Sometimes, SAS patrols in Borneo comprised as little as three men.

teams. Tactical unit size depends on the type of mission and type of insertion. For example, fast-boat and parachute operations may see a 10-man force or larger deployed, while using Swimmer Delivery Vehicles (SDVs) tends to limit the size of reconnaissance/underwater mission teams to four or six men. In fact, the limiting of team size by SDV deployment has become such a problem that the US Navy is attempting to overcome it in two ways. First, by the use of underwater shelters just off a beach within the operational area, which would serve as an underwater 'guerrilla' base and could be re-supplied covertly; second, with the proposed Advanced SEAL Delivery System, which will hold 10 SEALs.

Below: A US Green Beret. The basic operational unit of America's elite is the 12-man A Team, which packs a lot of firepower.

Russia's Spetsnaz also employs small tactical units. Spetsnaz brigades number around 400-1000 men. However, they are divided into 200-man *otryady*, each one of which is further split into three fighting companies and a signals company. During operations, though, a company would be further divided into three sections, each comprising three patrols of four or five men. 'Special mission teams' (invariably geared towards offensive tasks) may contain seven men – usually a commander, deputy commander, radio

operator, two reconnaissance men and two anti-tank/demolitions men.

Four-man patrols to 10-man teams or larger – these are the tactical units of today's elite forces. Each one suits the role of its parent unit, therefore it is impossible to say which is best. That said, it is worth bearing in mind that the British SAS has probably a wider range of roles than any other unit in the world, from counter-insurgency to operating behind the lines, and the four-man patrol is suited to them all.

What about firepower? It is a logical assumption that the bigger the unit the more firepower it will have. To a large extent this is correct. However, small-sized teams can pack a lot of punch and are not necessarily out-gunned in firefights.

Possessing heavy firepower is, on the face of it, an attractive proposition for a special forces team for several reasons. First, patrol members can lay down a large amount of firepower if they are ambushed, giving them a greater chance of escaping alive. Second, heavy firepower is useful for offensive actions, such as raids and ambushes. Third, it gives patrol members an increased sense of security. Fourth, it may persuade the enemy that he is fighting a large force, and thus prompt him to call off the engagement rather than risk heavy casualties.

On operations SAS four-man patrols are invariably heavily armed

We saw in the Weapons Skills Chapter that British SAS soldiers receive intensive training in the handling of a wide variety of small arms and support weapons. They are among the best in the world when it comes to reactively pointing and shooting weapons, and on operations four-man patrols are invariably heavily armed

During the Falklands campaign, for example, each patrol carried three assault rifles, one GPMG and four Browning High Power hand-guns. This meant each SAS trooper carrying three types of ammunition: 5.56mm for the assault rifles, 7.62mm for the GPMG (machine gun ammunition is traditionally distributed among patrol members) and 9mm for the handguns. The result was that each man was carrying in excess of 60kg, illustrating the major drawback with regard to foot patrols and firepower. This pales into insignificance when compared with the weight of kit being carried by SAS soldiers in the 1991 Gulf War. For example, members of the patrol codenamed Bravo Two Zero reportedly carried 95kg of equipment each! The weapons and quantities of ammunition carried by individual patrol members means that the SAS four-man patrol has excellent firepower. How do other units compare?

Right: A SEAL team on a fire and movement exercise. SEAL teams are generally larger than SAS units and more heavily armed.

Australian SAS teams are similarly equipped to their British counterparts when it comes to weapons. Because there is at least one Australian soldier more in the patrol there is probably a corresponding increase in firepower, but the difference is negligible.

The US Rangers, since they operate largely on foot, are also restricted in the main to light weapons. Ranger Combat Jeep Teams mount heavier weapons on their vehicles: two 7.62mm M60 machine guns, a 90mm M67 recoilless rifle, a 66mm M202A1 incendiary rocket launcher, a M72 LAW and Claymore mines. This ties in with the Ranger emphasis on firepower and support weapons. For example, the first wave of Rangers would probably parachute in and fight light with machine gun support until the landing zone or airfield was secure. Very quickly, successive waves would arrive, each of which would include jeep teams. In this scenario, however – attempting to seize and hold ground in the face of enemy resistance – the US Rangers are fighting more conventionally than would an SAS patrol.

The SEALs had to be rescued the next day by the Marines

The Green Beret 12-man A Team is, compared with the SAS four-man patrol, more heavily armed and has greater firepower, as do Spetsnaz units. However, the latter have a more tactically offensive role and require more firepower to fulfil their mission. Similarly, a 10-man SEAL detachment can pack a lot of punch, though all elite units require support services if engaging the enemy in a conventional firefight. During the 1983 US invasion of Grenada, for example, a SEAL detachment was despatched to rescue the governor-general of the island. However, after reaching Government House the SEALs became pinned down by Grenadan units, including three armoured personnel carriers, and had to be rescued the next day by an armoured formation of US Marines. A stark reminder of how

vulnerable lightly armed elite teams can be having lost the element of surprise.

On the face of it, therefore, the SAS four-man patrol is inferior in terms of firepower to other elite tactical formations. That said, the firepower of four SAS soldiers can be devastating in the first few seconds of an encounter, giving the enemy no indication of how many men he is

up against and allowing the patrol to withdraw. As SAS patrols are uninterested in holding ground, their firepower more than fulfils their needs. There is one more point to be made concerning firepower.

The wartime role of the SAS focuses on intelligence gathering. Patrols are expected to infiltrate unseen into enemy territory and establish covert observation posts (OPs), from where they can relay accurate and timely intelligence back to headquarters. A patrol operating in this way should not have to use its weapons: a patrol that has to use its weapons is considered to have failed in its task – i.e. it has allowed itself to be discovered by the enemy. Carrying this line of thought through to its logical conclusion, do

Above: As this photograph illustrates, Israeli Naval Commandos operate in small teams on operations, and they prefer to approach the target in dinghies.

SAS patrols behind the lines need their weapons? In other words, should not their fieldcraft skills be enough? The answer is obvious, but it is an interesting proposition nonetheless.

Small-sized teams have the potential to achieve results out of all proportion to their size, but only if their members possess a wide variety of skills. In the SAS there are only four patrol members to undertake a wide variety of tasks:

intelligence gathering, sabotage, 'hearts and minds' (see Counter-Insurgency Chapter) and long-range missions behind enemy lines. Team members must be able to use a wide variety of weapons (both friendly and hostile), treat themselves using field medicine techniques if injured, and be proficient in the handling of different types of military equipment.

Each member of an SAS four-man patrol is trained in at least one patrol skill, though he will probably be trained in more depending on his length of service with the Regiment. The blend of skills within a patrol gives it the greatest chance of being able function at its maximum potential when alone. The patrol skills are signalling, demolitions, medicine and languages. This mix did not arise by accident. When they are combined they make a small tactical unit a formidable military force.

Each SAS soldier will undoubtedly possess more than one patrol skill

Communications skills ensure that the patrol is able to keep in constant touch with headquarters. Language skills are among the most useful attributes possessed by an SAS patrol, and have had a major strategic impact upon campaigns. In Borneo, for example, many SAS troopers spoke Malay, which greatly facilitated communications with the jungle inhabitants. The subsequent bonds of trust and friendship formed between SAS and locals greatly helped the British war effort. Demolitions expertise is essential for sabotage operations behind enemy lines, such as those carried out during World War II.

Medical skills are also useful for a 'hearts and minds' campaign (see Counter-Insurgency Chapter). During the campaign in Oman (1970-76), for example, the work of the patrol medics was instrumental in gaining the trust of the Dhofaris.

Each SAS soldier will undoubtedly possess more than one patrol skill, and all will be trained in at least one troop skill (mountaineering and winter warfare, small boats and combat swimming, parachuting, and vehicles). This means that the four-man patrol will contain multi-skilled soldiers, perfectly equipped to undertake a variety of tasks.

How do other units compare with the SAS with regard to the blend of skills found in their tactical units? Analysis reveals that few other elite tactical units contain such diversity of skills as the

SAS four-man patrol does. Invariably, the Australian SAS closely mirrors its British counterpart. Each patrol will have individuals who have a variety of skills: radio operator, medic, tracker/scout and demolitions expert. The Australians, though, are geared towards the terrain of northern Australia and islands to the north. This means the skills pertaining to mountain and arctic warfare take a back seat.

US Ranger tactical units do not have the spectrum of skills possessed by SAS patrols, but they are not required to fulfil such diverse roles. The Rangers are the elite battalions of the US Army, trained, organised and equipped for long-range foot reconnaissance and raids. Their skills are therefore geared towards these tasks. As a result, the emphasis is on scouting and tracking, with signalling and weapons skills also being well to the fore in each six- or seven-man patrol.

Maritime units, such as the SBS, the SEALs and the Israeli Naval Commandos, are all highly trained, but their training is naturally geared towards their mission brief. For example, the SEALs are probably more highly trained than the SAS when it comes to medical skills and boats (see By Water Chapter), but they have no counter-insurgency role. Similarly, SBS patrol members will be just as expert as their SAS counterparts in underwater demolition and combat diving, probably more so, but they also have no counter-insurgency role.

Russia's Spetsnaz are orientated towards offensive action

The Green Berets, being trainers, necessarily have an excellent blend of skills within the 12-man A Team. As a team is expected to be able to establish indigenous units, it must have the means to set up an effective counter-insurgency campaign. Therefore, within each team is a medic, communications specialist, weapons specialists and engineers. However, compared with a four-man patrol they fall down regarding combat swimming and landborne insertion

Russia's Spetsnaz is orientated towards offensive action, and thus has little need for 'hearts and minds' skills. In wartime, for example, any captured enemy civilians or military

personnel that are reluctant to divulge information are tortured to reveal facts. Many consider this counterproductive, pointing out that Iraqi torture of SAS soldiers during the 1991 Gulf War proved useless, but this overlooks the fact that Spetsnaz soldiers will not capture elite troops on missions but clerks, second-line troops and the like. These people tend not to have

undergone resistance-to-interrogation training. Many Spetsnaz units have a single role, such as reconnaissance, surveillance and target acquisition, operating just behind the frontline. The Spetsnaz brigades acquitted themselves well in Afghanistan, though they did use torture and scorched-earth tactics. As a consequence of their heavy handed role, Spetsnaz seven-man teams

Left: A heavily armed SEAL team in the Mekong Delta during the Vietnam War. The firepower of small-sized units can often be devastating.

This translates into an ability to fulfil more tasks than any other elite tactical unit.

Turning now to flexibility, in previous chapters we have seen how SAS soldiers are trained and equipped to arrive at their target by air, sea and land. This gives them a great degree of tactical flexibility, which is also enjoyed by the SEALs, Spetsnaz and the Green Berets. However, there is another aspect to flexibility.

Daivd Stirling's ideas are still valid over 50 years later

SAS patrols, troops and squadrons can work as small or large units as needs arise. In Borneo, for example, SAS patrols frequently comprised only three men (this was because the Regiment was overstretched; nevertheless, the three-man patrol proved itself a workable concept), while in the 1991 Gulf War the Regiment deployed eight-man foot patrols, and during hostage-rescue operations SAS soldiers often work in two-man squads to clear rooms and buildings.

The small team has proved itself to be an integral part of special forces operations. Units such as the SAS, deliberately deploy small-sized teams so as to have the maximum effectiveness in wartime. Far from being a disadvantage, experience has shown that the SAS four-man patrol is a potent force in wartime.

The ability of SAS troopers to be flexible when it comes to working in tactical units of varying sizes means greater adaptability during operations. In a sense each SAS soldier is a self-contained operational unit, being multi-skilled and able to function on his own if necessary, such as when the rest of the patrol has been killed. Like most elite soldiers, he does not need an officer or NCO to tell him what to do. His thoughts are fluid and adaptable – this is what gives him the edge. Tactically, the SAS four-man patrol seems to be the most elite military unit when compared with those of other elite organisations. This is because its members are better than their special forces counterparts.

are very heavily armed and are well-equipped with explosives and mines. Compared with an SAS four-man patrol, though, they are poorly equipped for long-term intelligence gathering and parachute insertions (see By Air Chapter).

Overall, then, it can be seen that the SAS four-man patrol wins hands down when it comes to diversity of skills found within the patrol itself.

SELECTION AND TRAINING COURSES

Unit	Entry Qualifications	Selection	Post-Selection	Advanced Training
22 SAS	Volunteers must have served with a regular corps or regiment. In addition, they must have a minimum of three years and three months left to serve from the date that, if successful, they complete SAS Selection.	Run by Training Wing at Stirling Lines. Four-week course includes hill walking, navigation, physical training, marches and classwork. **Test Week**: six hill walking exercises in Elan Valley and Brecon Beacons. Culmination is 64km Endurance March. Weight carried by individuals ranges from 20-25kg plus personal weapon.	**Continuation Training:** (14 weeks) students are taught signalling, demolitions, combat medicine and survival skills. Ends with Escape and Evasion and RTI exercise. **Jungle Training:** (six weeks) ends in exercise that all must pass. **Parachute Course:** (four weeks) held at RAF Brize Norton. All students make eight jumps.	All 'badged' SAS soldiers receive intensive training in patrol skills (communications, medicine, languages and demolitions) and troop skills (combat diving and small boats, mountain warfare, parachuting and vehicle tactics). In addition, all troopers are rotated through CRW training at Stirling Lines.
Australian SAS	Several years service with parent unit. **Pre-selection:** 4-6 months with parent unit (running with bergens and brushing up on military skills).	**Week one:** basic fitness, assault course, physical tests, swimming test, weapons training, night navigation walks. **Week two:** must complete 14.5km run carrying 10kg load in under 90 minutes. **Week three:** 'Happy Wanderer' – 12-hour navigation walk and five-day endurance march carrying 50kg bergen. **SAS patrol course** **Parachute course**	**Reinforcement Training Cycle:** demolitions, weapons and survival skills. **Regimental Signaller's Course:** must be able to send and receive Morse at at least 10 words per minute. **Combat Medicine:** Army School of Health. **Troop Skills Training**: small boats, underwater swimming, freefall parachuting and vehicle driving.	Shooting, fieldcraft, land navigation and astro-navigation.

Unit	Entry Qualifications	Selection	Post-Selection	Advanced Training
Belgian Para-Commando Regiment	Basic medical and fitness tests.	**Phase one:** (three months) Commando Course. Basic soldiering combined with endurance training. **Phase two:** (one month) field training with an operational commando company. **Phase three:** (one month) parachute course.	None	**Equipes Spéciales de Reconnaissance:** long endurance marches carrying heavy bergens. Combat survival training, evasion and RTI. Advanced mountaineering training at the German Mountain Winter Warfare School.
Canadian Special Service Force (comprises Canadian Airborne Regiment; 1st Battalion, Royal Canadian Regiment; Royal Canadian Dragoons; 2nd Regiment, Royal Canadian Horse Artillery; 2nd Combat Engineer Regiment; 2nd Service Battalion; 2nd Field Ambulance; 2nd Military Police Platoon; 427 Tactical Helicopter Sqn)	Many SSF members are already airmobile-, parachute- or commando-qualified. Entry to Canadian Airborne Regiment – candidates must be able to survive the rigors of selection and must pass physical and weapons tests.	**Canadian Airborne:** (6-8 months) basic infantry and weapons skills training. **Parachute Course:** (three weeks) failures will go to other units of SSF, not the Airborne Regiment.	**Commando Course:** (two months) emphasis on speed and endurance with long forced marches and assault courses. Followed by mountain and arctic warfare training.	Helicopter drills, tactical parachuting, small patrols, navigation, commuications, field medicine, arctic and forest survival. Volunteers may undergo selection for the 42-man Reconnaissance Platoon (it is trained in HALO, HAHO, small boat insertions and counter-terrorism).
French Chasseurs Alpins	Strict medical with emphasis on anything that may impede cold weather and mountain operations. High level of fitness required to accommodate physiological changes associated with altitude.	**Basic Training:** (3-6 months) basic soldiering and training with weapons.	Further training with combat company, including support tactics for anti-tank and armoured support operations, helicopter deployment, climbing, cross-country skiing and abseiling.	**Specialist Course:** (6 months) students are taught high-altitude first aid, cold weather survival and navigation.

Unit	Entry Qualifications	Selection	Post-Selection	Advanced Training
French Foreign Legion	None	**Basic Training:** (three months) **First month:** drill, inspections. Marches with full military load: 10km (week one); 15km (week two); 20km (week three); and 60km (week four). **Second month:** weapons training, drill, forced marches, obstacle courses, including one 500m course to be completed in five minutes or less. **Third month:** mountain and winter warfare training. Tests include undertaking 200km mountain march in four days with full kit.	None	**2nd REP:** Candidates must pass para-commando course (parachute course, close-quarter battle training, endurance marches, signals, navigation, demolitions, small boats, jungle and mountain training). **Reconnaissance and Deep Action Commandos:** selection classified.
German Mountain Troops	Must pass medical and be suitable for high-altitude training.	**Basic Training:** (six months) infantry skills, mountain training (skiing, navigation), survival, cold weather first aid and patrolling.	None	None
Italian Alpine Troops	Fitness, self-motivated and skiing competence.	**Basic Training:** (three months) fitness training, drill and weapons training, tactics for taking and holding positions.	**Brigade Training:** (nine months) mountain training.	**Parachute Reconnaissance Company:** (three months) winter and mountain survival, climbing, abseiling, demolitions and weapons training. Parachute course, including static-line descents in the mountains.

Unit	Entry Qualifications	Selection	Post-Selection	Advanced Training
Parachute Regiment	Intelligence, self-motivation, initiative and a high level of fitness.	**P Company:** (16 weeks) **Weeks 1-4:** fitness training, runs, kit inspections. **Weeks 5-12:** field training, adventure training. **Weeks 13-15:** preparation for Test Week. Emphasis on team work. **Test Week:** individual and team events, culminating in Stretcher Race (12-man teams carrying 80kg stretcher for 1hr 20mins).	**Parachute Course:** (20 days)	**Pathfinder Platoon Selection: Weeks 1-2:** navigation and endurance walks, including 50km endurance march with 25kg load. Live firing, contact drills, assault courses. **Week 3:** four-day long-range reconnaissance patrol exercise.
Royal Marines	Intelligence, self-motivation, initiative and a high level of fitness.	**Basic Training:** (14 weeks) infantry skills, swimming, fieldcraft, navigation, helicopters and small boats. **Part 2:** (12 weeks) team training, infantry support weapons, seamanship. **Commando Course:** (four weeks) climbing, speed marches, 48km march across Dartmoor in full kit in eight hours.	None	**Mountain and Arctic Warfare Cadre: Pre-Selection:** (eight days) physical tests, climbing aptitude, trade tests. **Mountain Leader Course:** (18 months) cliff climbing, survival, RTI, communications, raids, combat medicine. Includes exercises in Scotland, Norway and Switzerland.
Special Boat Service	Must be a member of the Royal Marines	**Pre-Selection:** (two weeks) timed endurance walks, swimming with bergens, and testing suitability for diving. **Selection:** same as for SAS (see above).	**Training Course:** aptitude testing and trade training – beach surveys and photography, endurance canoeing, swimming exercises, small boat training, parachute descents at sea, maritime counter-terrorist skills.	

Unit	Entry Qualifications	Selection	Post-Selection	Advanced Training
US Green Berets	Must be airborne qualified, high school graduate and have passed Basic Training, Advanced Individual Training, Advanced Physical Readiness Test, junior NCO's course and be able to swim 50m in boots and uniform. Also vetted for security.	**Special Forces Assessment and Selection:** (three weeks) long-distance runs, bergen marches, confidence and obstacle courses. **Q Course Phase I:** (five weeks) patrolling, close combat, evasion, insertion, survival and land navigation. Tested over 12 consecutive nights in the wild.	**Q Course Phase II:** (five weeks) individual specialities training (weapons, explosives and demolitions, radios and medicine). **Q Course Phase III:** (four weeks) unconventional warfare and mission planning, followed by Exercise 'Robin Sage' (simulated insurgency exercise).	Region orientation with special forces group. Advanced training at Fort Bragg – sniping, HALO, HAHO, underwater swimming, operations and intelligence.
US Navy SEALs	Applicants must be qualified in a speciality, such as medical care, have passed a rigorous diving medical and have produced high scores on physical and mental aptitude tests.	**Basic Underwater Demolition Program:** **Weeks 1-4:** two-week warm-up, then small boat handling, beach recce and long-range patrol skills. **Week 5:** Hell Week. Physical and mental stamina tested with little sleep or food.	**Weeks 6-23:** specialist training, long swims and free-diving exercises, underwater and land demolitions. Students introduced to nuclear submarines, SDVs and limpet mines. Training ends with several small boat and swimming exercises. Static-line parachute course – students learn how to make wet drops into the sea with equipment.	Taught at Special Warfare Center and School, Fort Bragg. Students are taught most of the subjects found on Green Beret Selection. Further courses and training in deep reconnaissance, SDV driving, mini-submarines and bomb and mine disposal.
US Rangers	Medical Army Readiness Test	**Airborne Course:** (three weeks) for all those who are not parachutists. **Ranger Indoctrination Program:** (three weeks) infantry combat skills, reconnaissance, navigation. Ends with PT tests, timed runs and marches with full kit.	8-12 months with Ranger company, learning small unit tactics and basic combat skills.	**Ranger Course:** (eight weeks) physical tests, advanced patrol skills, demolitions, fire support, reconnaissance, survival and patrolling in different environments. Introduces students to airmobile and small boat operations.

THE WORLD'S PREMIER ELITE UNITS

Note: the following list does not include reserve or support units, unless where indicated.

Australia
1st Australian SAS Regiment (three squadrons)

Belgium
Para-Commando Regiment

Canada
Canadian Special Service Force (3000 personnel)

Egypt
Commando groups (seven)
Parachute brigade (one)

France
Chasseurs Alpins
Foreign Legion (8500 personnel)
Marine commandos (includes the Hubert combat swimmers)
Marine parachute regiments (four)
Parachute division (one)

Germany
1st Mountain Division (four battalions)

India
51st Independent Parachute Brigade (three parachute battalions and three para-commando battalions)

Indonesia
Amphibious para-commando reconnaissance unit (one)
Special Forces Command (3000 men)

Israel
Naval Commandos
Parachute Corps (includes the sayeret reconnaissance units)

Italy
Alpine troops (five brigades)
Combat swimmer unit (COMSUBIN)
Folgore Airborne Brigade
San Marco Marines

Jordan
101st Special Forces (three battalions)

New Zealand
New Zealand SAS Squadron

Netherlands
Marines Corps (2800 personnel)

North Korea
Special Purpose Corps (three commando, three airborne, one river crossing and four reconnaissance regiments; three amphibious, three airborne and 22 light infantry battalions)

Oman
Independent Reconnaissance Regiment (500 men)

Pakistan
Army Special Service Group (three battalions)

Russia
Fleet special forces brigades (four)
Naval Infantry (12,000 personnel)
Spetsnaz brigades (five – approximately 6500 personnel)

South Africa
Special forces infantry battalions (seven)

South Korea
'Capital Command' (12 brigades)

Spain
Spanish Legion (6400 personnel)
Special operations battalions (six)

Syria
Special forces regiments (eight)

Thailand
Royal Thai Special Forces (two divisions)

United Kingdom
22 SAS Regiment (four squadrons)
Parachute Regiment (three battalions)
Royal Marines (includes Special Boat Service, 539 Assault Squadron and Comacchio Group)

United States
82nd Airborne Division (three airborne and one airborne artillery brigades)
101st Airborne Division (nine rifle, three light artillery, one engineer and one air defence battalions)
US Air Force squadrons to support special operations (13)
US Army 75th Ranger Regiment
US Army Delta Force (four squadrons)
US Army Special Forces Groups (five)
US Marine Corps (183,000 personnel)
US Navy SEAL Teams (six)
US Navy Swimmer Deliver Vehicle Teams (two)

PREMIER COUNTER-TERRORIST UNITS

Unit strengths are given when known and for those formations that are dedicated counter-terrorist formations. An asterisk indicatesss that counter-terrorism forms only one aspect of a unit's responsibility.

Europe
Comacchio Group (United Kingdom)
    Strength: 400
Escadron Spécial d'Intervention (Belgium)
    Strength: 200
Gendarmerie Special Unit (Austria)
    Strength: 200
GEO (Spain) Strength: 120
GIGN (France) Strength: 50
Groupe Interventional Speciale (Italy)
    Strength: 46
GSG 9 (Germany) Strength: 200
Jandara Suicide Commandos (Turkey)
    Strength: 150
NOCS (Italy) Strength: 50
SAS (United Kingdom) *
SBS (United Kingdom) *
Whiskey Company, Royal Dutch Marines
    (Netherlands) Strength: 113

United States
Delta Force *
FBI Hostage Response Team
    Strength: 50
Nuclear Emergency Search Team
    Strength: unknown
SEAL Team 6 Strength: 183

Rest of the World
Army Commando Squadron (Sri Lanka)
    Strength: unknown
Army Puma Unit (Ecuador)
    Strength: 200
Australian SAS (Australia) *
Aviations Security Commando (Philippines)
    Strength: unknown
Counter-Terrorist Special Attack Unit
    (South Korea) Strength: 80

Detachment 81 (Indonesia)
    Strength: 100
Emergency Response Team (Canada)
    Strength: 300
Falcon 8 (Argentina)
    Strength: 45
Grupo de Operaciones Especiales (Chile)
    Strength: 50
Light Reaction Force (Philippines)
    Strength: 120
National Guard (Saudi Arabia) Strength: 40
New Zealand SAS (New Zealand) *
Projecto Talon (Brazil) Strength: 30
Police Special Action Units (Japan)
    Strength: unknown
Police Special Duties Unit (Hong Kong)
    Strength: 100
Police Special Task Force (Oman) Strength: 300
Police Tactical Team (Singapore) Strength: 100
SATGAS ATBARA (Anti-Skyjacking Task
    Force) of the Indonesian Air Force
    (Indonesia) Strength: unknown
SATGAS GEGANA (Counter-Terrorist Task
    Force) of the Indonesian National Police
    (Indonesia) Strength: 100
Sayeret Matkal (Israel) Strength: 200
707th Special Battalion of the Army Special
    Warfare Command (South Korea)
    Strength: only 120 men are actually trained
    for hostage-rescue missions
Special Action Unit (Malaysia) Strength: 50
Special Counter-Terrorist Unit (India)
    Strength: 100
Special Intervention Brigade (Venezuela)
    Strength: unknown
Special Operations Group (Colombia)
    Strength: unknown
Special Services Group (Pakistan)
    Strength: 175
Special Strike Unit (Malaysia)
    Strength: 50
Special Task Force (South Africa)
    Strength: unknown
Sultan's Special Force (Oman) Strength: 500

INDEX